GOOGLE CLOUD
ANTHOS

A DEFINITIVE HANDBOOK

BY

NAVVEEN BALANI

RAJEEV HATHI

GOOGLE CLOUD ANTHOS

A DEFINITIVE HANDBOOK

By Navveen Balani, Rajeev Hathi

Dec 2021: First Version

TABLE OF CONTENTS

CHAPTER 3 : ANTHOS CLUSTERS ON BARE METAL

43

CHAPTER 1 : ANTHOS IN A NUTSHELL

Cloud computing kept the business and remote workforces connected during this ongoing Covid pandemic. As we move into 2022, every organisation would eventually adopt cloud models and existing cloud businesses would look at ways to streamline their processes for better business continuity.

Broadly, in addition to the standard single public cloud deployment model, there are 3 kinds of cloud models we are talking about - multi-cloud deployment, hybrid cloud deployment and cloud on the edge.

A Multi-cloud environment enables enterprises to modernise their applications and adopt cloud services from multiple cloud vendors based on their business requirements and avoid a single cloud vendor lock-in. As workloads and infrastructure are different for each enterprise, this approach gives a flexibility to deliver applications on different cloud providers based on customer's cloud preference, regulations, cost factors, disaster recovery strategy, user locality, specific cloud services and at the same time being agile and cloud neutral.

A Hybrid cloud environment provides an environment where applications are deployed on a public cloud as well as on-premises or on-prem data centers. Organisations having existing on-prem investments usually adopt the hybrid deployment model to start extending their on-prem infrastructure to the cloud and building effort towards modernising their applications (like creating cloud-native applications).There is also a common scenario where customer data residing in an on-prem data center cannot leave the geographical boundaries due to compliance and regulations reasons and hybrid model is adopted to scale on-prem infrastructure to public cloud and also leverage cloud services to run non-sensitive functions or tasks. Also, adopting a hybrid cloud model brings in a new set of roadmap for enterprises to consolidate their on-prem infrastructure, migrate and modernise applications, reduce operational overheads and improve their deployment processes. This strategy can also help large enterprises to reduce the existing carbon footprint of their IT infrastructure and move towards carbon-aware cloud regions and deployments.

A Cloud on the Edge deployment model is driven by use cases where data and compute needs to be located closer to end-users. In a connected world and with 5G gaining momentum (and the talks around Metaverse), the next generation applications would drive new set of requirements like near real-time decision making, low latency streaming, gaming and virtual experience, immersive experience and collective intelligence. With adoption of Internet of Things (IoT), every object in the world would have the potential to connect to the Internet and provide their data so as to derive actionable insights on its own or through other connected objects. To realise this vision for IoT, Edge computing would play a very critical role. Industries need to be agile and prepared for this kind of transformation.

For example, in a virtual shopping mall, one can 'try' outfits using the concept of digital mirrors/changing rooms. Fashion advisor bots can suggest outfits based on your persona, can provide the same real-life experience in future. Similarly, there is also a great opportunity in the e-learning spectrum to transform education and the entire on-line learning experience to be immersive, interactive and more conducive/friendly for students.

All of the above use cases would require applications to be deployed on the edge to provide real-time, immersive and interactive experiences.

As organisations start to transition towards these cloud models, the following questions arise -

- How to create cloud applications that can be deployed anywhere?

- How to deploy and manage cloud applications in a consistent way across these environments?

- How to modernise existing on-prem applications leveraging the existing virtualised infrastructure?

- How to extend single cloud deployment to support multi-cloud deployments?

- How to provide consistent compliance and security policies across environments?

- How to provide the same consistent tooling for continuous integration and continuous deployment across environments?

To address the above challenges in a consistent way, we need a platform that enables organisations to build cloud applications that can be deployed anywhere - multi-cloud, hybrid or cloud on the edge and managed using a single unified interface.

INTRODUCING GOOGLE ANTHOS

Google Anthos is a modern application management platform that provides a consistent development and operations experience for cloud and on-prem environments.

As per Google Cloud documentation, Anthos provides the following high level capabilities -

- Build, deploy, and optimise applications anywhere—in a simple, flexible, and secure way.

- Provides consistent development and operations experience for hybrid and multi-cloud environments.

- Protect applications and software supply chain.

Basically, the Anthos gives you a consistent platform and toolset to address the questions that we had listed in the earlier section.

Let's understand the key components of Anthos.

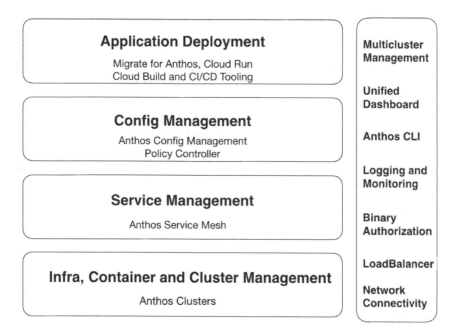

Figure 1.1: Anthos Platform - Component Overview

Infra, Cluster and Container Management

Containers have pretty much become the de-facto standard or approach to package and deploy software applications on the cloud. Containers package all the required dependencies and abstracts software applications from their base runtime environment, allowing you to build and deploy applications on any operating environment that provides a container management platform.

Container management platforms are available with all operating platforms (Windows, Mac, Linux) and virtually all cloud vendors offer managed services for running the containers. Hence containers have become the de-facto choice to run software applications in a consistent way across all environments.

Google provides the managed Kubernetes distribution called Google Kubernetes Engine (GKE) for container orchestration and management, handling upgrades and offers enterprise grade capabilities like workload security, pod autoscaling, audit logging etc.

Anthos platform leverages GKE for both on-prem and multi-cloud deployment. With Anthos, you can get a reliable, standardised and secured way to run your workloads on GKE clusters in any environment. You can also monitor your workloads and enforce policies on your GKE clusters across environments in a unified way.

Anthos is supported on on-premises through VMware vSphere or through bare metal installation. On the multi-cloud front, both AWS and Azure cloud provide support for Anthos.

For a list of deployment details, please refer to Deployment Options with Anthos section.

Service Management

One of the architecture patterns for breaking down a large monolithic application is a collection of loosely coupled fine-grained services (microservices) and packaging them as independent deployable units using containers and exposing the functionality through APIs. All communications between the services happen through the APIs.

With the microservices architecture style implemented, there are various cross cutting concerns that also need to be implemented, such as securing communication between services, collecting telemetry data, logging and monitoring, API throttling, traffic management, version management etc. These functions can be decoupled from the actual application by employing a technology called Service Mesh. Service Mesh at its core adds a sidecar proxy container alongside your primary workload container, and intercepts all the requests to inject the above mentioned cross cutting concerns in a unified way. Open source tools like Istio provide these capabilities uniformly across a network of services.

Anthos provides Anthos Service Mesh (ASM), which is a managed service mesh offering that inherits features from Istio and provides various other enterprise capabilities, operation agility and management of services across the Anthos environments.

The figure 1.2 shows the component of Anthos Service Mesh.

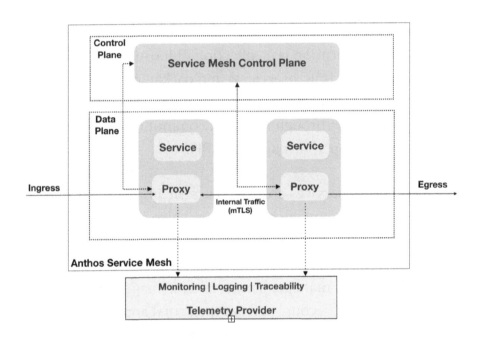

Figure 1.2 - Anthos Service Mesh - Component Overview

The ASM control plane provides functions like centralised service discovery, encryption, authentication and authorisation, traffic management and network security policies for your services. The data plane is served by a proxy runtime that gets installed as a sidecar container along with your services in each pod as part of the service mesh installation. You can also selectively inject the sidecar for required pods based on the namespaces. All communication between services happens through the proxy sidecar which works in conjunction with the service mesh control plane to provide networking, security and other functions like telemetry, traceability and controlling application traffic flow. The sidecar injects these functions seamlessly without requiring any code modification to your services.

Once the data from your services are captured, the ASM provides deep visibility for your microservices and their network interaction, allowing you to define and monitor service level objectives (SLOs). Using this feature, you can define the required service level indicators (SLIs) like latency, availability etc. and define thresholds for each of your services and generate alerts to take corrective action if there is a breach of threshold value. For example, login service should be available 99.5% of the time or say, view order service should not have > 200ms response time latency.

The figure 1.3 shows the snippet of Anthos Service Mesh dashboard where you can select the SLI and define the SLO and can test your compliance against actual service data.

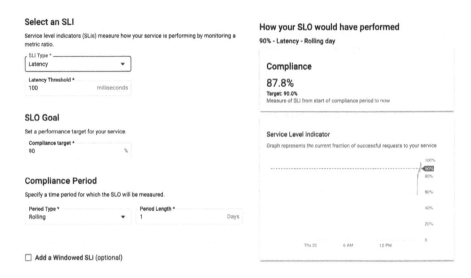

Figure 1.3 - Anthos Service Mesh - SLI/SLO Overview

ASM is supported on on-prem, bare metal and multi-cloud environments. However certain features of ASM differs between the supported platforms, for example, currently at the time of this writing, Cloud Monitoring is not available on VMware and Bare metal and you can use third party tools like Prometheus, Kiali, and Grafana dashboards to enable monitoring for your environment.

Please refer to Google Cloud documentation for latest supported features. For more details on service management, check out the excellent resource (https://sre.google/sre-book/introduction/) from Google's SRE book.

We will go over ASM in greater depth, covering installation and deployment of the same, later during the course of this book

Anthos Config Management (ACM)

One of the common challenges faced by enterprises is how to ensure deployment configurations are always consistent with the required desired state across environments (hybrid and multi cloud) and can be audited and monitored whenever required. That's where Anthos Config Management (ACM) comes into play which allows us to define configurations, policies and custom rules in a centralised place, which is then applied and enforced to all the required GKE clusters, across environments, to provide the required desired state.

The figure 1.4 shows the architecture for Anthos Config Management.

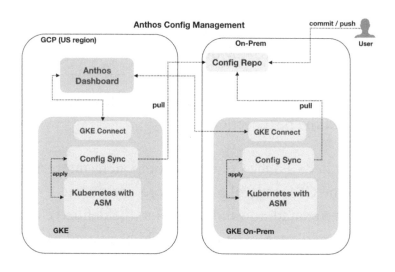

Figure 1.4 - Anthos Config Management Architecture

A central Git repository acts as a single source of truth for all the deployment configurations. The config repository in the above diagram holds all the configurations. The repository can be deployed at a location where it can be accessed from all your environments. For a hybrid environment, the repository would be typically hosted on-prem to leverage existing access control and any audit requirements.

ACM provides a set of components that ensures any configuration changes committed to the Git repository is applied to all the clusters and validated from time to time. These components need to be installed on all the required GKE clusters.

The key components of ACM includes:

- Config Sync – The Config Sync component synchronises config files in the config repository by applying them on the respective GKE clusters. Any difference between the actual state of the GKE cluster and stored configuration is actively monitored and reconciled. We will go through a use case of Config Sync in the next section.

- Policy Controller – Policy Controller component intercepts requests to the GKE control plane before any cluster resources are updated, to validate against the defined cluster policies for compliance. The policy could be related to security or any custom business rules that must be implemented as part of the governance. The Policy Controller component blocks any changes to the clusters that don't comply with the defined policies.

- Config Connector – Config connector is an add-on component that allows you to create and manage Google Cloud services like BigQuery, Compute Engine etc. using Kubernetes. It offers in-built Custom Resource Definition (CRDs) objects that manage Google Cloud resources that you create using config manifest files.

- Binary Authorization - Binary Authorization service is an optional component that can be enabled and configured to ensure only trusted container images are deployed in the GKE cluster. Many enterprises allow only verified images to be installed which pass their information security requirements and image scan policies and by applying the Binary Authorization configuration, the required images can be signed and verified during deployment.

As shown in the ACM architecture diagram, the ACM Operator is installed in all GKE Clusters. The operator uses the Config Sync agent to pull the configuration from the Git repository and convert the configurations into objects that can be applied to the GKE Cluster. The operator periodically checks if the status of the cluster matches the configuration and reconciles them. For instance, if you accidentally delete a namespace from the cluster that exists in the configuration, you will see that the deleted namespace is automatically created and restored back on the cluster.

We will cover the use case of ACM in detail later during the course of this book.

ACM Repository configuration

As you already know now how ACM helps sync config repo with the cluster to keep it in desired state. But how do you structure your repo? One of the important considerations is how to structure your configurations that need to be applied to your clusters. There are two documented ways to deal with configs in the repo - unstructured and hierarchical.

The unstructured repo follows no conventions and you can organise the content of the repo in the way you want. This can give you a lot of flexibility and is often recommended for most users. If you are already having an existing repo then you can continue to follow the unstructured path. The unstructured repository can also be used where you are using existing third party tools like Helm and want to expand the Helm charts or maintain ad hoc deployment configurations.

For hierarchical repos, the Config Sync component requires the configuration in the Git repository to be in a certain directory structure as shown in figure 1.5.

In order to understand the structure, let's take an example of a use case where you want to apply certain configurations and policies to specific clusters based on location [on-prem and on cloud US or India region] and environment [dev or prod].

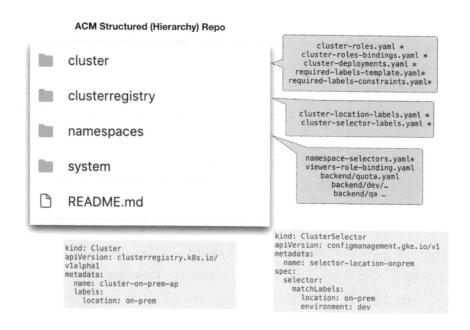

ACM Structured (Hierarchy) Repo

cluster

> cluster-roles.yaml *
> cluster-roles-bindings.yaml *
> cluster-deployments.yaml *
> required-labels-template.yaml*
> required-labels-constraints.yaml*

clusterregistry

> cluster-location-labels.yaml *
> cluster-selector-labels.yaml *

namespaces

> namespace-selectors.yaml*
> viewers-role-binding.yaml
> backend/quota.yaml
> backend/dev/...
> backend/qa ...

system

README.md

```
kind: Cluster
apiVersion: clusterregistry.k8s.io/
v1alpha1
metadata:
  name: cluster-on-prem-ap
  labels:
    location: on-prem
```

```
kind: ClusterSelector
apiVersion: configmanagement.gke.io/v1
metadata:
  name: selector-location-onprem
spec:
  selector:
    matchLabels:
      location: on-prem
      environment: dev
```

Figure 1.5 - Anthos Config Management Directory Structure

Firstly you will define namespaces to provide logical segregation of application workloads. The namespaces can be based on application tiers or environments - for example, frontend, backend, development, production etc. The namespace configurations are stored in *namespaces* directory.

Secondly you would need to identify the clusters where you need to apply certain configurations or policies. The configuration for selecting a particular cluster is stored in *clusterregistry* directory. You would typically apply a label to tag the required cluster - for example, location:on-prem for clusters that are in on-prem environment and use the ClusterSelector configuration to select the clusters that match the label as shown in the above figure.

The ClusterSelector configuration is not active until you reference it in the required configuration. For example, if you create a ClusterRole config that defines certain permissions as per your use case, you can have config only applied to a specific cluster by providing the following annotation with the value as the name of the ClusterSelector resource - configmanagement.gke.io/cluster-selector: <name-of-the-clusterselector-resource>.

There is also a simplified way of selecting the cluster if you do not want to use the *ClusterSelector* config. You can simply put the following cluster selector annotation in the config that you want to be applied to that cluster, for example configsync.gke.io/cluster-name-selector: cluster1, cluster2. The said annotation will apply the config to cluster1 and cluster2.

All cluster specific configurations like *ClusterRole* or *ClusterRoleBinding* are kept in the *cluster* directory. By default the configs placed in the cluster directory are applicable to all the clusters unless you use the above mechanism of using cluster selector annotation or *ClusterSelector* config.

The *system* folder holds system configurations which are used by the ACM operator, like how to sync the repository and its version.

We would revisit the concepts in detail when we setup ACM for our use case later during the course of the book.

Application Development and Deployment

For developing applications on Anthos, Google Cloud offers various integrated tool sets that simplify development, integration and deployment.

One of them is Google Cloud Code service that lets you write, run and debug your cloud native application and provides a set of predefined templates that helps deploying applications quickly. The service provides a complete development environment and can integrate with leading development IDE tools like IntelliJ and Visual Studio code.

There is another such service called Cloud Build that lets you create a standardised build workflow to compile, test and verify codebase and build container images. The workflow can be triggered upon code commits to the source control repository. Cloud Code is integrated with Cloud Build to generate production builds for deployment.

Cloud Build also integrates with ACM at build time to ensure any new deployment artifacts (Kubernetes resources) are validated well in advance against existing policies. Once changes are validated, deployment changes are propagated to the production environment.

The above services and its seamless integration with the Anthos ecosystem ensures continuous integration and continuous delivery (CI/CD) practice can be easily adopted for building secure and compliant Anthos applications.

We will cover the use case of Cloud Build and CI/CD later in the *CI/CD with Anthos* chapter.

DEPLOYMENT OPTIONS WITH ANTHOS

The deployment options of Anthos can be primarily bucketed into the following three categories -

• Hybrid cloud deployment

• Multi cloud deployment

• Edge deployment

Hybrid cloud deployment

In a Hybrid deployment model, you have your own existing on-prem data center infrastructure which is extended to the cloud. The question we ask is why extend it to the cloud? Apart from the cost factor, the dynamic nature of the cloud itself is the biggest motivation to embark on a journey to the cloud.

The organisations today are looking at multiple consistent ways to be agile and deliver modern applications quickly. Based on their cloud adoption and transformation, the enterprises can be at various stages such as -

- Infrastructure modernisation - In process of consolidating and optimising their infrastructure.

- App Modernisation – In process of modernising or evolving their applications by moving towards cloud native solutions for faster deployment and agility.

- Extending their workloads to cloud – Looking to extend their on-prem infrastructure to cloud for better optimization, scalability or running non-sensitive workloads.

With any of the above given stages, organisations need a unified way to develop and manage applications at scale, across on-prem and cloud environments.

Based on what technologies the customer uses and where they are in their cloud journey, the following two Anthos offerings can be adopted:

- Anthos clusters on VMware

- Anthos on Bare Metal

Anthos clusters on VMware

Customers who have existing on-prem investments in VMware vSphere and want to leverage capabilities offered by GKE to create, manage and deploy containers or migrate their virtual machines to native containers, they can start with Anthos clusters on VMware offering.

This could be a good starting point to consolidate and modernise the existing infrastructure where containers can reside on-prem and be managed effectively using Anthos GKE clusters and later migrate the required workloads to the cloud if necessary.

New development workloads, possibly non-sensitive, can be moved to the cloud and optimised to make use of the auto scaling feature of the cloud. The entire on-prem infrastructure can be managed through Cloud Console and security policies can be rolled out for GKE clusters hosted on both on-prem and cloud.

Enterprise can also use Migrate for Anthos service offering to convert the whole virtual machine into containers that can be deployed directly to Anthos clusters.

Anthos on Bare Metal

Customers who run physical servers (without the overhead of

virtualization) as part of their existing enterprise infrastructure, can rely on Anthos on Bare Metal offering to deploy Anthos applications directly on their hardware infrastructure.

Anthos clusters on bare metal can be centrally managed using the Google Cloud console (through Connect) and perform monitoring and logging through Cloud Monitoring. This gives the same unified capabilities of managing and monitoring like any other Anthos cluster on the cloud with improved performance, security cost and direct control of the applications running inside your own enterprise infrastructure.

Edge deployment

We discussed some of the use cases for edge applications, like virtual fashion shopping and immersive online-education earlier. In order to realise these applications, we need capabilities like localised compute and data storage, ultra-low latency and bandwidth, to provide near real-time experiences to end users.

One way of realising this is to leverage Anthos Clusters on Bare metal offering and deploy applications directly on your own bare metal servers, at your edge locations. closer to end users.

Leveraging Anthos on Bare Metal provides you the capability to run Anthos applications on your edge locations and also provide central management through a unified way.

Multi cloud deployment

One of the strategic decisions that enterprises need to take is how they can be cloud-agnostic. This can be due to various drivers that include cost model, customer affinity towards a particular cloud vendor, availability of cloud regions, disaster recovery strategy or compliance and regulations. Going forward, we will see multi cloud support would be a key strategic decision being adopted by many enterprises.

With Anthos, you can have your workloads running in AWS, Azure and Google Cloud and get a unified view and deployment experience across these cloud environments.

We will explore creating a GKE cluster on AWS and how it can be seamlessly managed using Google Cloud console, later during the course of this book.

SUMMARY

In this chapter, you went through the core capabilities of Google Anthos platform and various deployment options supported by it.

Anthos enables you to develop cloud-native applications and allows you to build applications that can be deployed anywhere – hybrid, multi cloud or edge in a secure and consistent way.

Selecting a deployment strategy is specific to each enterprise, based on their requirements and choosing Anthos provides a flexible option to modernise, transform, build or extend the infrastructure to create scalable, secured, transparent and compliant applications across environments in a unified way.

In the next chapter, you will look at setting up Anthos on Google Cloud.

CHAPTER 2 : ANTHOS INSTALLATION

In this chapter, we will go through the steps to install Anthos on Google Cloud. Anthos setup requires that you have the following prerequisites in place:

- Google Cloud project

- Anthos APIs are enabled. It will allow you to use Anthos features. You can enable Anthos API for your project by login into **Google Cloud Console**. From the navigation menu, select *APIs & Services > Dashboard*. Click *Enable APIs and Services*. Click *Google Enterprise APIs* category from the left panel and you should see *Anthos*. Click on the same and enable APIs.

- The command line tool – gcloud. You will get this by installing Cloud SDK

As part of installation, you will setup the following:

- Setup a GKE Cluster

- Register the cluster for Anthos

- Setup Anthos Service Mesh (ASM)

- Setup Anthos Config Management (ACM)

SETTING UP A GKE CLUSTER

Follow the steps below to set up the GKE Cluster.

Creating Service Account

As a first step, you will create a service account that will be used by the cluster node VMs.

```
gcloud iam service-accounts create gke-anthos —
project=${PROJECT_ID}

gcloud config set project ${PROJECT_ID}

gcloud projects add-iam-policy-binding ${PROJECT_ID}
—member="serviceAccount:gke-anthos@$
{PROJECT_ID}.iam.gserviceaccount.com" \
—role="roles/owner"

gcloud iam service-accounts keys create gke-anthos-
key.json \
```

```
--iam-account=gke-anthos@$
{PROJECT_ID}.iam.gserviceaccount.com \
--project=${PROJECT_ID}
```

The above command creates a service account named *gke-anthos* and is assigned the *owner* role, that grants full admin access to the said account. For our use case here, we are simplifying the access privilege by granting the owner permission. But in an ideal world, granting owner role is not recommended and the principle of least privilege should be followed when granting permissions to users or service accounts. (For more details on managing service accounts, please refer to Google Cloud Reference documentation - https://cloud.google.com/iam/docs/best-practices-for-using-and-managing-service-accounts)

The second command will create and download the JSON key for the said service account.

Creating a GKE cluster

You will create a GKE cluster with two 4 vCPU nodes and the machine type as *e2-standard-4*.

```
gcloud container clusters create anthos-cluster \
--zone=asia-southeast1-a \
--machine-type=e2-standard-4 \
```

```
--num-nodes=2 \
--service-account=gke-anthos@$
{PROJECT_ID}.iam.gserviceaccount.com \
--scopes=https://www.googleapis.com/auth/cloud-
platform \
--workload-pool=${PROJECT_ID}.svc.id.goog
```

The above command will create the cluster named *anthos-cluster* in *asia-southeast1-a* (Singapore) zone that will use a regular release channel of GKE. The cluster has a workload identity enabled that will allow Kubernetes service accounts to represent the Google Cloud IAM service accounts.

Registering the cluster

The above created GKE cluster must be registered with the project fleet or Hub thereby allowing you to view and manage the cluster from the Anthos console dashboard.

```
gcloud container hub memberships register anthos --
gke-cluster=asia-southeast1-a/anthos-cluster --
enable-workload-identity
```

The above command registers the *anthos-cluster* cluster and creates a membership named *anthos*. The registration process will install the Connect Agent on the cluster that will enable you to view and manage your cluster from the Anthos dashboard. The Connect Agent will authenticate to Google using the above created service account JSON key. Registering a cluster indicates that the cluster is now in the realm of Anthos ecosystem.

SETTING UP ANTHOS SERVICE MESH (ASM)

This section will demonstrate how to set up Anthos Service Mesh (ASM). ASM setup requires that you have the following client tools as a prerequisites:

- git
- kpt
- kubectl
- jq

Download and Install

As a first step, you will download the ASM installation script. The script will validate the cluster so that it meets ASM requirements and automates all the steps that are required to install ASM.

```
curl https://storage.googleapis.com/csm-artifacts/
asm/asmcli_1.12 > asmcli
```

At the time of writing this book, the latest ASM version is
1.12. The above command downloads the latest ASM
installation script and redirects the content to the file named
asmcli. The *asmcli* file is then made an executable script file
using the following command.

```
chmod +x asmcli
```

The executable script file is then used to install ASM.

```
./asmcli install \
--project_id {PROJECT_ID} \
--cluster_name anthos-cluster \
--cluster_location asia-southeast1-a \
--ca mesh_ca \
--output_dir <your_dir_path> \
--enable_all
```

The above command installs the ASM with default settings.
The Certificate Authority used is Mesh CA. Mesh CA is a
Google managed private certificate authority that issues
certificates for mutual TLS authentication within the service
mesh. The *output_dir* is where the script downloads the asm
packages and Istio command line tool *istioctl* that can be used

to customise the installation and also to debug and diagnose the mesh. The *enable_all* option enables the required Google APIs needed to install ASM and set IAM permissions.

Once ASM is installed successfully, you will see two additional namespaces in the cluster, viz. asm-system and istio-system.

```
kubectl get ns
```

Output:
```
NAME               STATUS    AGE
asm-system         Active    3m1s
istio-system       Active    4m42s
```

Enable the Sidecar Proxy

Once the installation is complete, the control plane component *istiod* will contain a label containing ASM revision tag. This revision tag will be used to enable the automatic injection of sidecar proxy containers. The below commands will show the ASM revision tag:

```
kubectl -n istio-system get pods -l app=istiod --
show-labels
```

Output:
```
istiod-asm-1120-4-dd5489f55-txhkq Running 0
55s app=istiod,install.operator.istio.io/owning-
resource=unknown,istio.io/rev=asm-1120-4 ...
```

```
istiod-asm-1120-4-dd5489f55-z9mqq Running 0
app=istiod,install.operator.istio.io/owning-
resource=unknown,istio.io/rev=asm-1120-4 ..
```

As seen from the above output, the ASM revision tag
is *asm-1120-4*.

ASM provides mesh functionality through the use of sidecar
containers or envoy proxies (or proxy containers). The sidecar
container runs alongside your primary container in the same
pod. As part of ASM installation, you have to enable the
automatic injection of sidecar proxy. It effectively means you
have to label your namespaces with the above ASM revision tag
that will spin up a proxy container alongside your main
container as part of that namespace.

```
kubectl label namespace <namespace> istio-injection-
istio.io/rev=<asm-revision> --overwrite
```

The above command will ensure that your pods will now have
a mesh proxy container alongside its primary container. If the
pods are already running, then you have to restart the pods to
trigger the injection.

INSTALLING INGRESS GATEWAY

The earlier version of ASM, by default, had the gateway service as part of *istio-system* namespace. The new version of ASM does not come with ingress gateway and must be installed separately. As a best practice, you should use a separate namespace for deploying the gateway.

Note: If you need the earlier default behaviour of prior ASM versions, you should include --option legacy-default-ingressgateway as part of asmcli intsllation.

In this section, you will install the ingress gateway as part of ASM in the *demo-gateway* namespace. ASM ingress gateways are services that provide load balancing functionality for your service mesh.

As a first step, create the namespace for ingress gateway.

```
kubectl create namespace demo-gateway
```

You will now enable auto-injection of sidecar proxy for workloads as part of the above namespace. You already learned in the previous section how to enable auto-injection of sidecar proxy. You can follow similar steps.

```
kubectl label namespace demo-gateway \
   istio.io/rev=asm-1120-4 --overwrite
```

You will apply an ingress gateway configuration located in the <your_dir_path>/samples/gateways/istio-ingressgateway/ directory. The <your_dir_path> was created as part of asmcli installation earlier. This will deploy necessary resources and setup the ingress gateway service that can be used as default istio gateway for external traffic.

```
kubectl apply -n demo-gateway
-f <your_dir_path>/samples/gateways/istio-
ingressgateway
```

You would see the following output.

```
poddisruptionbudget.policy/istio-ingressgateway
created
horizontalpodautoscaler.autoscaling/istio-
ingressgateway created
role.rbac.authorization.k8s.io/istio-ingressgateway
created
rolebinding.rbac.authorization.k8s.io/istio-
ingressgateway created
service/istio-ingressgateway created
serviceaccount/istio-ingressgateway created
```

SETTING UP ANTHOS CONFIG MANAGEMENT (ACM)

This section will demonstrate how to set up Anthos Config Management (ACM). ACM setup requires that you have the following prerequisites in place:

- Any known source code repo like Git or Google Cloud Source Repository (this will be used by Config Sync to sync with clusters)

- nomos client tool (Optional tool)

As part of installation, you will perform the following:

- Setup Config Sync

- Setup Policy Controller

Setting up Config Sync

Config Sync lets you deploy configurations and security policies consistently across multiple Kubernetes clusters and namespaces spanning hybrid and multi-cloud environments. The config files are stored as part of a source repository like Git and its current state in the repo is synced with multiple clusters where Config Sync is enabled.

As a first step you will enable ACM APIs.

```
gcloud beta container hub config-management enable
```

You will then download and apply the Custom Resource Definition (CRD) manifest that will represent the Config Sync operator resource.

```
gsutil cp gs://config-management-release/released/
latest/config-management-operator.yaml config-
management-operator.yaml
```

The above command will download the CRD manifest file. You will then apply the said manifest file.

```
kubectl apply -f config-management-operator.yaml
```

You will provide the Config Sync operator with the read-only access to the source code repo. The way you do this is by setting up the authentication type. If your repo allows read-only access without any authentication then you do not have to do anything special and just specify 'none' as authentication type.

The following authentication types are supported:

- SSH key pair

- cookiefile (only supported by Google Cloud Source Repositories)

- Token based

- Google service account (only supported by Google Cloud Source Repositories)

The authentication type you choose will depend on the kind of source code repo that you have setup. Most repos will support SSH based authentication. It is a universal and recommended way of authenticating with a repo. For our setup, you will use SSH based authentication in order for the Config Sync operator to access the source code repo.

You will create a SSH key pair.

```
ssh-keygen -t rsa -b 4096 \
-C "<repo-user-name>" \
-N '' \
-f <path-to-key-file>
```

The above command creates a 4096-bit RSA key. The user name is the one that will be used by the Config Sync operator to authenticate with the repo. You will also specify the path where the key pair files will be generated. The key pair will include a private and a public key. Register the public key with your source code repo. Every repo will have its own way of recognising the public key. You can refer to the documentation of your source code repo to understand how to register the public key. (*Note: Config Sync does not support SSH key passphrase*)

You will now create a Kubernetes Secret that will contain your private key. The Secret must be created in the `config-management-system` namespace and named as *git-creds*.

```
kubectl create ns config-management-system && \
kubectl create secret generic git-creds \
--namespace=config-management-system \
--from-file=ssh=<path-to-private-key>
```

The above command creates the secret named *git-creds* in the `config-management-system` namespace. You have to specify the path where your private key is stored.

You will now create a custom resource named *ConfigManagement* as defined by the above created Config Sync operator CRD and apply it to the cluster. This will allow us to tune or configure the behaviour of the Config Sync.

You can write the following manifest file as follows.

```
# config-management.yaml
apiVersion: configmanagement.gke.io/v1
kind: ConfigManagement
metadata:
  name: config-management
spec:
```

```
cluster: anthos-cluster
sourceFormat: unstructured
git:
  syncRepo: <repo-url>
  secretType: ssh
```

The above configuration enables Config Sync for our cluster.

You must specify the URL of the repo and the secret type as SSH as we used the same as our authentication type.

You can apply the above manifest to the cluster using the following

```
kubectl apply -f config-management.yaml
```

You can use the tool called nomos to verify the Config Sync installation.

```
nomos status
```

The above command will validate if the Config Sync operator is installed successfully or not. A status
of PENDING or SYNCED indicates a successful installation.

Later in the ACM Chapter, we would also look at how to configure ACM through the Google Cloud console and leverage the capabilities of ACM using a sample application.

Setting up Policy Controller

Policy Controller is a way to audit and enforce the compliance for your cluster through a well defined programmable policies. These policies are also called guardrails that lay down the rules which guard the configuration of the resource against any changes or updates that may indicate or reflect a security violation.

It is very easy to set up the Policy Controller for your cluster. All you need is to change the above created *config-management.yaml* file to enable the Policy Controller.

```
apiVersion: configmanagement.gke.io/v1
kind: ConfigManagement
metadata:
  name: config-management
spec:
cluster: anthos-cluster
sourceFormat: unstructured
  policyController:
    enabled: true
  git:
    syncRepo: <repo-url>
    secretType: ssh
```

The above highlighted snippet enables the Policy Controller. Apply the manifest file and the Policy Controller will be installed.

You can also verify the installation.

```
gcloud beta container hub config-management status \
    --project=PROJECT_ID
```

Output:
```
Name            Status   Last_Synced_Token  Sync_Branch
Last_Synced_Time      Policy_Controller
anthos-cluster  SYNCED   a687c2c                 1.0.0
2021-02-17T00:15:55Z  INSTALLED
```

If the output has the value *INSTALLED* under the column *Policy_Controller*, it means Policy Controller is successfully enabled.

SUMMARY

In the chapter, you went through the installation of Google Anthos and installed all the key components of Anthos on Google Cloud.

In the next chapter, we will demonstrate Anthos GKE setup on the Bare Metal servers.

CHAPTER 3 : ANTHOS CLUSTERS ON BARE METAL

In Chapter 1, we went through the Anthos architecture, its core components and the deployment model supported by Anthos.

In this Chapter, we will describe one of the key Anthos offering – **Anthos clusters on bare metal** and go about installing Anthos GKE clusters directly on bare-metal servers running Ubuntu OS.

We will also cover the deployment models supported by Anthos GKE clusters on bare metal and deploy a sample container-based application to demonstrate end-to-end functionality.

ANTHOS CLUSTERS ON BARE METAL OVERVIEW

Anthos clusters on bare metal allows you to install Anthos GKE clusters directly on bare metal servers thereby allowing you to use and exploit capabilities of GKE in your environment in an on-prem data center.

Enterprises can deploy and run cloud-native/container applications directly on GKE clusters running in their own environment on supported hardware and operating systems, without the overhead of any virtualised environment.

The GKE clusters can be centrally managed using the Google Cloud console (through Connect) and leverage the central monitoring and logging capabilities through Cloud Logging and Monitoring service. Running Anthos clusters directly on your own infrastructure, gives the same capabilities as that of managing and monitoring Anthos on the cloud. You get improved performance, security, cost reduction and direct control over the applications as it is running inside your own infrastructure.

Anthos Clusters on Bare metal allow enterprises to deploy data and compute workloads at the edge locations – closer to end-users or systems, to realise use cases that require ultra-low latency capabilities or near real-time decision making.

With IoT and 5G gaining momentum, in the future we would see new class of applications that will require new set of capabilities like near-real time decision making, ultra-low-latency, streaming applications, immersive and 3D experiences and the whole notion of collective intelligence where humans and system would learn from each other.

Industries need to be agile and be prepared for such transformation in future. For instance, various industrial automation use cases like condition based monitoring, predictive maintenance, using Augmented Reality/Virtual Reality (AR/VR) for inspecting the manufacturing plants etc, all require edge computing to process data at the edge and take corrective actions quickly. Similarly, consumer driven use cases like using digital mirrors for trying apparel outfits, use of AR/VR applications for immersive online education in schools/university, connected environment use cases (like connected home, connected cars etc.), Metaverse solutions - all would require applications running on the edge to provide real-time and true connected experience.

With Anthos clusters on Bare Metal, all the above use cases can become a reality and you can leverage the same unified capabilities of Anthos platform to build, deploy, manage, secure and govern cloud-native applications at the edge location.

Next we will look at how to install Anthos clusters on bare metal.

ANTHOS CLUSTERS ON BARE METAL INSTALLATION OVERVIEW

In this section we will go through the prerequisite, deployment overview and set up Anthos clusters on Bare metal.

Hardware and Operating Systems requirements

Anthos clusters on bare metal requires a minimum hardware configuration to run on a supported Linux operating system.

The Linux operating system currently supported are CentOS (8.1 and 8.2), RHEL (8.1 and 8.2) and Ubuntu (18.04 and 20.04). In this Chapter, we will be installing Anthos clusters on Ubuntu 20.04. (Please refer to the Anthos on bare metal documentation for latest support on operating system. - https://cloud.google.com/anthos/clusters/docs/bare-metal/latest/installing/os-reqs)

With respect to hardware requirements, we require a minimum of 3 machines to install Anthos clusters on bare metal , but in real-world you would need at least 5 machines for high availability and resiliency. We look at the deployment topology of these machines in the next section.

The minimum hardware configurations required are 4 CPUs, 32 GB RAM and 128 GB storage. (Please check the documentation for latest supporting requirements - https://cloud.google.com/anthos/clusters/docs/bare-metal/latest/installing/hardware)

DEPLOYMENT OVERVIEW

With bare metal topology, you can define four types of clusters:

- Admin cluster – Admin cluster manages user clusters. It is used to create, update, delete user clusters. It consists of only control plane nodes where management components are deployed. Admin clusters also hold service account keys to access required google services and ssh keys for remote cluster management.

- User cluster - The user cluster runs your workloads. It consists of control plane nodes (for managing the cluster and its state) and worker nodes which executes the workload or applications.

- Hybrid cluster - The hybrid cluster plays a dual role of both admin and user. It serves as a meta control plane and also runs workloads.

- Standalone cluster - The standalone cluster is a non-admin cluster that only runs user workloads. It can be primarily used as an edge server for edge devices with high resource constraints.

Anthos clusters on bare metal supports three deployment models – Standalone, Multi-cluster and Hybrid deployment model. Based on the deployment model, you can choose from the above mentioned cluster type for running and managing workloads.

The Standalone deployment model is a single cluster that serves as both admin cluster as well as user cluster. This type of deployment model lets you manage every cluster independently and it's preferred when you need strict isolation from other clusters, say, due to compliance requirements.

The Multi-cluster deployment consists of one admin cluster and multiple user clusters. This type of deployment lets you manage multiple user clusters. This model is preferred, where you have multiple projects/teams with different workload requirements that need to be executed independently, but centrally managed securely through the admin cluster.

The Hybrid cluster deployment is similar to a multi-cluster deployment, with the ability to run user workloads on the admin cluster also. This deployment model gives the flexibility to reuse your admin cluster environment, to run additional workloads based on your infrastructure usages.

Deployment Topology

The figure 3.1 shows the deployment topology with a HA control plane.

Anthos for bare metal user cluster deployment topology at its basic can have one master node and one worker node. It also has a load balancer which serves the ingress traffic. You can choose to have either a bundled load balancer or an external load balancer. With a bundled load balancer, you can have it placed in the control plane node or it can be part of a dedicated node or node pools.

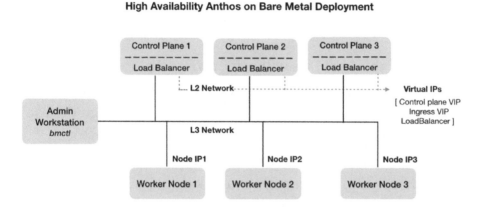

Figure 3.1 - HA Deployment for Anthos Cluster on Bare metal

The load balancer node(s) is configured with Virtual IPs for control plane to send traffic to GKE Kubernetes API server and for ingress traffic to workloads (services). The only requirement for the bundled load balancer nodes is that they all have to be on the same layer 2 (L2) subnet. The L2 subnet is required as the load balancer announces its Virtual IPs (VIPs) via Address Resolution Protocol (ARP) broadcasts. The worker nodes don't have any restriction on the L2 subnet and can reside in the regular L3 subnet. You can also have a bastion host or admin workstation to connect to cluster nodes for performing security and management related operations.

The cluster and load balancer nodes are setup using the manifest configuration file. If you want to have a more resilient highly available (HA) deployment topology, you can set up three control plane and worker nodes. That will ensure that your cluster nodes will always be available in the event of a node failure.

As part of this book, we will demonstrate Anthos for bare metal use case using non-HA deployment topology. The setup will simulate bare metal or physical machines through the use of virtual machines (VMs). You will use Google Compute Engine (CE) service to create VMs. In an ideal world though, you will perform bare metal set up using physical machines in a HA environment. We will keep it simple for our use case and focus more on understanding concepts and how you can create and configure bare metal clusters.

The figure 3.2 shows the topology that we would be setting it up.

The deployment topology consists of one control plane node with a bundled load balancer and two worker nodes. The workstation nodes as shown in the diagram above have connectivity to all the nodes. In the workstation node you will install the required client tools like *kubectl* and docker.

You will also install the *bmctl* tool that is required to install Anthos clusters on the cluster nodes.

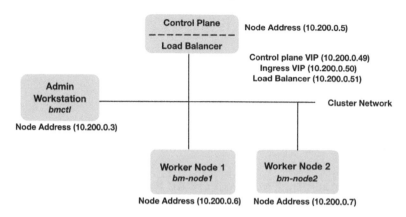

Figure 3.2 - Non-HA Deployment for Anthos Cluster on Bare metal

In the next section, we will look at the prerequisite, followed by how to set up the required topology.

INSTALLING ANTHOS CLUSTERS ON BARE METAL

In this section, you will learn how to install Anthos clusters on bare metal using virtual machines (VMs).

Installation Prerequisite

Based on the topology described in the earlier section, we need four machines with the following identical configuration.

OS – Ubuntu 20.0.4

CPU/vCPUs – 4 core

RAM – 32 GB

Storage – 128 GB

To set up the machines, you will create four VMs in Google Cloud with the above configuration. One VM will be the workstation node, let's keep the node name as *bm-wkst*. Another VM will be used as a control plane node, let's refer to this as *bm-cp* and the rest two VMs will be the worker nodes, let's call this as *bm-node1* and *bm-node2*.

If you are planning to set up a bare metal cluster in another cloud provider, you can do so with the same set of prerequisites and there is nothing different you have to do.

Most cloud virtual networks operate at layer 3 (L3). With bare metal setup, there is a requirement to set up a L2 subnet for our bundled load balancer. As we are simulating the setup on Google Cloud, we will also have to simulate the L2 network. We will create an L2 network through the use of Virtual Extensible LAN (VXLAN) technology. VXLAN is a tunneling protocol that encapsulates L2 frames within an L3 packet. As our bundled load balancer (control plane node) requires an L2 network, for simplicity we will have all the four cluster nodes connected on the L2 subnet.

In a non-cloud environment, typically in a physical data center you already have access to the L2 network.

Installation Plan

The following are the high-level steps that you will perform to set up bare metal topology –

- Create VPC

- Configure Firewall

- Create 4 VMs with required configuration

- Install software prerequisite on the workstation machine (*bm-wkst*)

- Setup SSH for passwordless connections between the workstation (bm-wkst) and the cluster node machines. (*bm-cp, bm-node1* and *bm-node2*)

- Create VXLAN between all the four VMs to simulate L2 subnet

- Execute the *bmctl* tool for creating bare metal cluster configuration file.

- Modify the bare metal cluster configuration file based on our topology/environment

- Create the hybrid cluster using the modified configuration file

- Validate the deployment

- Login and authenticate the cluster in Google Anthos dashboard

- Verify the cluster details in Google Anthos dashboard

- Deploy a sample application and invoke it via Load Balancer URL

The first step, creating the VPC is an optional step and is used to isolate the VM environments. You can use your existing or default VPC to setup the virtual machines.

(Note- The setup described below is covered in detail as part of Anthos Playlist on youtube – https://www.youtube.com/playlist?list=PL42TJmsjarLcV_dSupNmgzNZbAnlJnww) (Kindly refer to Episode 6 in the series).

Create VPC

Go to Google Cloud console and create a VPC, named *bm-vpc*

with subnet IP range 10.0.0.0/20 and your preferred region.

We have selected the *us-east* region as there is enough quota available in the region, which is required as per the installation prerequisite. If you don't have sufficient quotas, kindly request for the same to the Google Cloud Support.

The figure 3.3, shows the snapshot of VPC configuration.

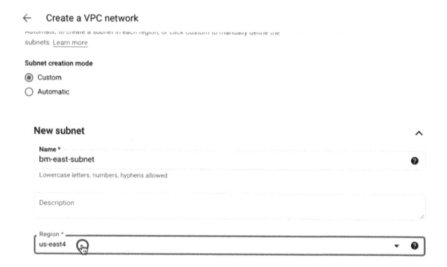

Figure 3.3 - VPC Configuration

Configure Firewall

Configure firewall to allow the port for internal and external communication for the VPC (bm-vpc) network created in earlier step. Create the following three ingress entries as part of firewall rule creation with the details as shown in the figure 3.4.

Name	Type	Targets	Filters	Protocol/ports	Requirements
bm-allow-external	Ingress	Appy to all	IP range: 0.0.0.0/0	tcp:80,8080,443	Allow external clients to communicate over standard ports
bm-allow-internal	Ingress	Appy to all	IP range: 10.0.0.0/20	tcp:0-65535 udp:0-65535 icmp	Broad range for ports to allow for internal communication between cluster and load balancer nodes. For exact port detail, refer to Anthos bare metal network configuration documentation.
bm-allow-ssh	Ingress	Appy to all	IP range: 0.0.0.0/0	tcp:22	SSH communication to the workstation and cluster nodes

Figure 3.4 - Firewall Configuration Details

The Figure 3.5, shows the snapshot of the firewall dashboard in Google Cloud.

	Name	Type	Targets	Filters	Protocols / ports	Action	Priority	Network ↑	Logs
☐	bm-allow-external	Ingress	Apply to all	IP ranges: 0	tcp:80,8080,443	Allow	1000	bm-vpc	Off
☐	bm-allow-internal	Ingress	Apply to all	IP ranges: 1	tcp:0-65535 udp:0-65535 icmp	Allow	1000	bm-vpc	Off
☐	bm-allow-ssh	Ingress	Apply to all	IP ranges: 0	tcp:22	Allow	1000	bm-vpc	Off

Figure 3.5 - Firewall Details in Google Cloud

Create VMs

Next, create the four identical VMs with the following configuration -

Machine Configuration:

For machine type and region, enter the following details as shown in figure 3.5.

Machine type: ec2-standard-8 (8vCPU, 32GB Memory)

Region: Select the same region as your VPC region (in this case us-east4)

Boot disk: For boot disk, select Ubuntu OS, version as 20.04 TLS   and boot disk size as 128GB as shown in figure 3.6.

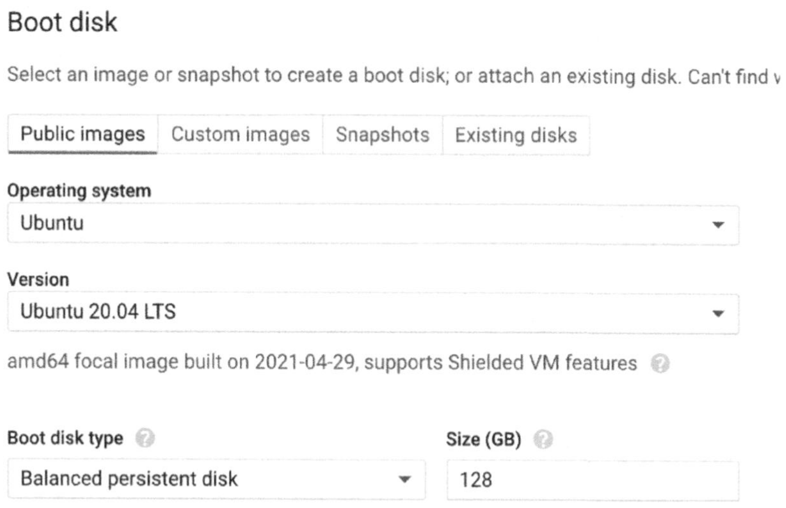

Boot disk

Select an image or snapshot to create a boot disk; or attach an existing disk. Can't find v

| Public images | Custom images | Snapshots | Existing disks |

Operating system

Ubuntu

Version

Ubuntu 20.04 LTS

amd64 focal image built on 2021-04-29, supports Shielded VM features

Boot disk type   Size (GB)

Balanced persistent disk   128

Figure 3.6 - OS and Disk Configuration

Next, add the machine to your VPC as shown in the figure 3.6.

- Click Networking

- Edit Network interfaces and change network to your VPC (i.e bm-vpc) and leave the rest of the default values as shown in figure 3.7.

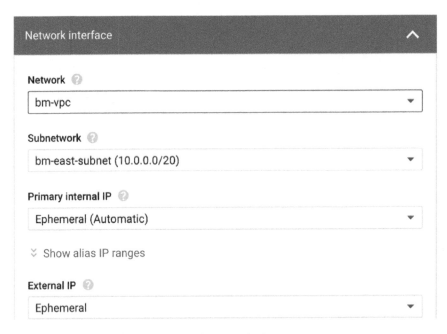

Figure 3.7 - Network Details for VM

- Click Create to Create the VM.

Follow the earlier steps to create the rest of the 3 VMs.

Once completed, you should have four VMs as shown in the figure 3.7.1

Name ↑	Zone	Recommendations	In use by	Internal IP
bm-cp	us-east4-c			10.0.0.5 (nic0)
bm-node1	us-east4-c			10.0.0.6 (nic0)
bm-node2	us-east4-c			10.0.0.7 (nic0)
bm-wkst	us-east4-c			10.0.0.3 (nic0)

Figure 3.7.1 - VM Details

Install software on workstation machine

SSH into the workstation machine (bm-wkst). On the command prompt, carry out the following steps

1. Stop and disable AppArmor and verify the same (as it's not supported by Anthos on bare metal) by issuing the following commands.

```
sudo systemctl stop apparmor

sudo systemctl disable apparmor

sudo systemctl status apparmor | grep "Active"

# Active: inactive (dead) since Sun 2021-04-04
13:06:18 UTC; 19s ago
```

2. Disable Ubuntu firewall and verify the same. (as it's not supported by Anthos on bare metal) by issuing the following commands.

```
sudo ufw disable
```

```
sudo ufw status
# Status: inactive
```

3. Install Docker 19.03+ and verify the same by executing the following commands

```
sudo apt-get update
```

```
sudo apt-get install \
  apt-transport-https \
  ca-certificates \
  curl \
  gnupg-agent \
  software-properties-common \
  docker.io
```

```
sudo docker version
```

You should see version as 19.03.x and above in the output. Add your user to the docker group to run docker as a non-root user (required by bmtcl tool).

```
sudo usermod -aG docker $USER
```

4. Download and install kubectl tool by executing the following commands

```
curl -LO "https://storage.googleapis.com/
kubernetes-release/release/$(curl -s https://
storage.googleapis.com/kubernetes-release/
release/stable.txt)/bin/linux/amd64/kubectl"
```

Execute the following command to make it executable and copy it to bin folder

```
chmod +x kubectl
```

```
mv kubectl /usr/local/sbin/
```

5. Install bmctl tool and verify by executing the following commands

```
mkdir baremetal
```

```
cd baremetal
```

```
gsutil cp gs://anthos-baremetal-release/bmctl/
1.7.0/linux-amd64/bmctl .
```

```
chmod a+x bmctl

mv bmctl /usr/local/sbin/

bmctl -v
```

Setup SSH for passwordless connections between workstation and cluster machines

In this step, you will setup SSH connection between workstation node and cluster machines.

1. Go to the workstation node *bm-wkst* and type the following command to create authentication pairs for SSH. Do not enter any passphrase while generating the keys.

    ```
    ssh-keygen -t rsa
    ```

2. Go to the control panel node *bm-cp* and enable SSH access for root login. Follow the steps and enter the command as highlighted in bold below.

    sudo su

    passwd

```
New password:
Retype new password:
passwd: password updated successfully
```

Note down the above password, as you would need this to login to the *bm-cp* node from the workstation node *bm-wkst*.

3. Next, edit the *ssh_config* file to allow root login and password authentication.

   ```
   nano /etc/ssh/sshd_config
   ```
   Uncomment the fields - *PermitRootLogin* and *PasswordAuthentication* and provide value as yes as shown below and save the changes.

   ```
   PermitRootLogin yes

   PasswordAuthentication yes
   ```

4. Restart the ssh service.

   ```
   service sshd restart
   ```

5. Go to the workstation node *bm-wkst* and execute the *scp* command to copy the public key to *bm-cp* node.

   ```
   scy -i ~/.ssh/id_rsa root@<internal-ip>
   ```

Replace the placeholder with the internal IP address of your *bm-cp* node. (You will get the internal IP address from the Google Cloud VM dashboard)

6. Similarly, enable SSH access for root login on *bm-node1* and *bm-node2* nodes and copy the public key from *bm-wkst* to both the said nodes.

Create VXLAN between all the four VMs for L2 subnet

In this step, we would create the VXLAN between all the nodes.

We will be binding the following VXLAN IP address to the workstation and cluster nodes

Node Name	VXLAN IP Address	Bridge connections
bm-wkst	10.200.0.2/24	\<bm-cp-ipaddress> \<bm-node1-ipaddress> \<bm-node2-ipaddress>
bm-cp	10.200.0.3/24	\<bm-wkst-ipaddress> \<bm-node1-ipaddress> \<bm-node2-ipaddress>

bm-node1	10.200.0.4/24	<bm-wkst-ipaddress> <bm-cp-ipaddress> <bm-node2-ipaddress>
bm-node2	10.200.0.5/24	<bm-wkst-ipaddress> <bm-cp-ipaddress> <bm-node1-ipaddress>

Keep a note of the internal IP address allocated to the above nodes as we will be using it during the command execution below. You can get the internal IP address for the nodes from the Google Cloud VM dashboard.

1. Next, SSH to the *bm-wkst* node and execute the following command one by one, to create the VXLAN between *bm-wkst* and cluster machines.

```
set -x

sudo ip link add vxlan0 type vxlan id 42 dev
ens4 dstport 0

sudo bridge fdb append to 00:00:00:00:00:00
dst <bm-cp-ipaddress> dev vxlan0

sudo bridge fdb append to 00:00:00:00:00:00
dst <bm-node1-ipaddress> dev vxlan0
sudo bridge fdb append to 00:00:00:00:00:00
dst <bm-node2-ipaddress>dev vxlan0
```

```
sudo ip addr add 10.200.0.2/24 dev vxlan0

sudo ip link set up dev vxlan0
```

2. Next, SSH to the *bm-cp* node and execute the following command one by one to create the VXLAN between *bm-cp* node and other machines.

```
set -x

sudo ip link add vxlan0 type vxlan id 42 dev
ens4 dstport 0

sudo bridge fdb append to 00:00:00:00:00:00
dst <bm-wkst-ipaddress> dev vxlan0

sudo bridge fdb append to 00:00:00:00:00:00
dst <bm-node1-ipaddress> dev vxlan0

sudo bridge fdb append to 00:00:00:00:00:00
dst <bm-node2-ipaddress>dev vxlan0

sudo ip addr add 10.200.0.3/24 dev vxlan0

sudo ip link set up dev vxlan0
```

3. Next, SSH to the *bm-node1* node and execute the following command one by one, to create the VXLAN between *bm-node1* and other machines.

```
set -x

sudo ip link add vxlan0 type vxlan id 42 dev
ens4 dstport 0

sudo bridge fdb append to 00:00:00:00:00:00
dst <bm-wkst-ipaddress> dev vxlan0

sudo bridge fdb append to 00:00:00:00:00:00
dst <bm-cp-ipaddress> dev vxlan0

sudo bridge fdb append to 00:00:00:00:00:00
dst <bm-node2-ipaddress>dev vxlan0

sudo ip addr add 10.200.0.4/24 dev vxlan0

sudo ip link set up dev vxlan0
```

4. Next, SSH to the *bm-node2* node and execute the following command one by one to create the VXLAN between *bm-node2* and other nodes.

```
set -x
```

```
sudo ip link add vxlan0 type vxlan id 42 dev
ens4 dstport 0
sudo bridge fdb append to 00:00:00:00:00:00
dst <bm-wkst-ipaddress> dev vxlan0

sudo bridge fdb append to 00:00:00:00:00:00
dst <bm-cp-ipaddress> dev vxlan0

sudo bridge fdb append to 00:00:00:00:00:00
dst <bm-node1-ipaddress>dev vxlan0

sudo ip addr add 10.200.0.5/24 dev vxlan0

sudo ip link set up dev vxlan0
```

This completes setting up the VXLAN across all the nodes.

Next, we will use *bmctl* tool for creating bare metal cluster
configuration file

Execute bmtcl for creating bare metal cluster configuration file

The *bmctl* tool is a command-line tool for creating Anthos
clusters on bare metal. The tool can automatically set up the
necessary Google service accounts and enables required Google
Service APIs for Anthos clusters on bare metal installation.

Follow the steps for running the *bmctl* tool -

1. First, authenticate with Google Cloud with your credentials, so you can create and manage service accounts by issuing the following command.

    ```
    gcloud auth login --update-adc
    ```

2. Once authenticated, set your Google Cloud project ID. It is good to have *Editor* or *Owner* permission for your project.

    ```
    gcloud config set project <project-id>
    ```

3. Next execute the *bmctl* tool to generate the deployment artifacts that will be used for installing the cluster.

    ```
    bmctl create config -c bm-cluster-demo \
    --enable-apis --create-service-accounts --
    project-id=<project-id>
    ```

The above command will enable the relevant service APIs for the project, create service accounts with the required roles for the project access and create the configuration file for cluster setup in *bmctl-workspace/bm-cluster-demo/* folder as shown in figure 3.8.

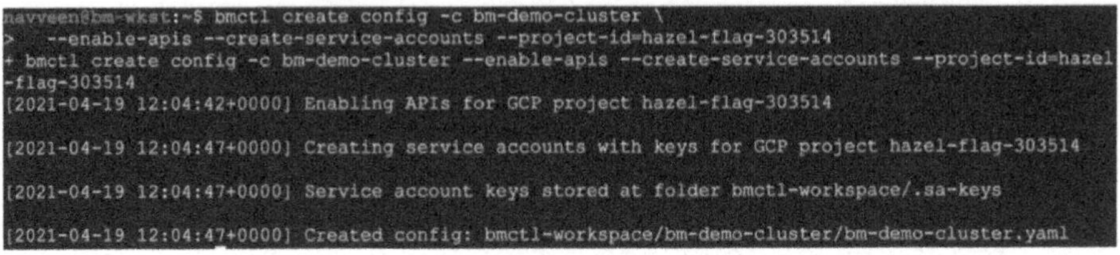

Figure 3.8 - bmctl create config command output

4. Next edit the generated *bmctl-workspace/bm-cluster-demo/bm-cluster-demo.yaml* file. Follow the lines highlighted in bold, it will provide information or instructions to change as per your setup.

```
## bm-cluster-demo.yaml

# bmctl configuration variables.
gcrKeyPath: /home/navveen/bmctl-workspace/.sa-keys/
hazel-flag-303514-anthos-baremetal-gcr.json
sshPrivateKeyPath: /home/navveen/.ssh/id_rsa
#change this to the path where you have created the
ssh key.
---
apiVersion: v1
kind: Namespace
metadata:
  name: cluster-bm-demo-cluster
#This is name of cluster, you can change or leave
this as is
---
apiVersion: baremetal.cluster.gke.io/v1
kind: Cluster
```

```
metadata:
  name: bm-demo-cluster
  namespace: cluster-bm-demo-cluster
spec:
  # Cluster type. This can be:
  #   1) admin:  to create an admin cluster. This
can later be used to create user clusters.
  #   2) user:   to create a user cluster. Requires
an existing admin cluster.
  #   3) hybrid: to create a hybrid cluster that
runs admin cluster components and user workloads.
  #   4) standalone: to create a cluster that
manages itself, runs user workloads, but does not
manage other clusters.
  type: hybrid
  #change type to hybrid.
  # Anthos cluster version.
  anthosBareMetalVersion: 1.7.0
  # GKE connect configuration
  gkeConnect:
    projectID: hazel-flag-303514
    #Project id that we had specified earlier, leave
this as-is
  # Control plane configuration
  controlPlane:
    nodePoolSpec:
      nodes:
      - address: 10.200.0.3
```

#Change address to ip address of the control plane node – 10.200.0.3, that we had configured as part of VXLAN earlier

```
# Cluster networking configuration
clusterNetwork:
  # Pods specify the IP ranges from which pod networks are allocated.
  pods:
    cidrBlocks:
    - 192.168.0.0/16
  # Services specify the network ranges from which service virtual IPs are allocated.
  # This can be any RFC1918 range that does not conflict with any other IP range in the cluster and node pool resources.
  services:
    cidrBlocks:
    - 10.96.0.0/20
# Load balancer configuration
loadBalancer:
  mode: bundled
  # Load balancer port configuration
  ports:
    # Specifies the port the load balancer serves the Kubernetes control plane on.
    # In 'manual' mode the external load balancer must be listening on this port.
    controlPlaneLBPort: 443
```

This address must not be in the address pools below.
    controlPlaneVIP: 10.200.0.49
    #change Control Plane VIP to 10.200.0.49, based on our VXLAN configuration

IngressVIP specifies the VIP shared by all services for ingress traffic.
This address must be in the address pools below.
    ingressVIP: 10.200.0.50
    #Change – Uncomment ingressVIP and change Ingress Plane VIP to 10.200.0.50, based on our VXLAN configuration
AddressPools is a list of non-overlapping IP ranges for the data plane load balancer.
    addressPools:
    - name: pool1
      addresses:
Each address must be either in the CIDR form (1.2.3.0/24)
or range form (1.2.3.1-1.2.3.5).
      - 10.200.0.50-10.200.0.70
#Change – Uncomment addressPools and add Load Balancer IP ranges 10.200.0.50-10.200.0.70 based on our VXLAN configuration
A load balancer node pool can be configured to specify nodes used for load balancing
    clusterOperations:

```
# Cloud project for logs and metrics.
projectID: hazel-flag-303514
# Cloud location for logs and metrics.
location: us-central1
---

# Node pools for worker nodes
apiVersion: baremetal.cluster.gke.io/v1
kind: NodePool
metadata:
  name: node-pool-1
  namespace: cluster-bm-demo-cluster
spec:
  clusterName: bm-demo-cluster
  nodes:
  - address: 10.200.0.4
  - address: 10.200.0.5
#Change address to IP address of our worker nodes -
10.200.0.4 and 10.200.0.5 based on our VXLAN
configuration
```

5. Save the file and exit the editor.

6. Next create the cluster by running the following command

```
bmctl create cluster -c bm-demo-cluster
```

The *bmctl* runs various preflight checks on your environment to ensure it meets the hardware specifications, network connectivity between cluster machines, verifying that load balancer node is on L2 network and other conditions to ensure that Anthos cluster can be created as per the deployment configuration.

The *bmtcl* tool takes a while to run (approximately 30 - 45 minutes) and following messages will be displayed as shown in figure 3.9.

```
navveen@bm-wkst:~$ bmctl create cluster -c bm-demo-cluster
+ bmctl create cluster -c bm-demo-cluster
Please check the logs at bmctl-workspace/bm-demo-cluster/log/create-cluster-20210419-121403/create-
cluster.log
[2021-04-19 12:14:13+0000] Creating bootstrap cluster... OK
[2021-04-19 12:16:01+0000] Installing dependency components... OK
[2021-04-19 12:18:43+0000] Waiting for preflight check job to finish... OK
[2021-04-19 12:23:43+0000] - Validation Category: machines and network
[2021-04-19 12:23:43+0000]        - [PASSED] node-network
[2021-04-19 12:23:43+0000]        - [PASSED] 10.200.0.3
[2021-04-19 12:23:43+0000]        - [PASSED] 10.200.0.3-gcp
[2021-04-19 12:23:43+0000]        - [PASSED] 10.200.0.4
[2021-04-19 12:23:43+0000]        - [PASSED] 10.200.0.4-gcp
[2021-04-19 12:23:43+0000]        - [PASSED] 10.200.0.5
[2021-04-19 12:23:43+0000]        - [PASSED] 10.200.0.5-gcp
[2021-04-19 12:23:43+0000]        - [PASSED] gcp
[2021-04-19 12:23:43+0000] Flushing logs... OK
[2021-04-19 12:23:44+0000] Applying resources for new cluster
Waiting for cluster to become ready: System Services Deployment, GKE Connect
```

Figure 3.9 - bmctl create cluster command output

Verify the deployment

Once the *bmtcl* tool is successfully executed, you can verify the cluster status by executing the following command.

```
kubectl --kubeconfig bmctl-workspace/bm-demo-
cluster/bm-demo-cluster-kubeconfig get nodes
```

You would see the nodes and status as running as shown in figure 3.10, denoting a successful installation of the cluster.

```
navveen@bm-wkst:~$ kubectl --kubeconfig bmctl-workspace/bm-demo-cluster/bm-demo-cluster-kubeconfig get nodes
NAME        STATUS   ROLES     AGE    VERSION
bm-cp       Ready    master    48m    v1.19.7-gke.1200
bm-node1    Ready    <none>    43m    v1.19.7-gke.1200
bm-node2    Ready    <none>    43m    v1.19.7-gke.1200
navveen@bm-wkst:~$
```

Figure 3.10 - cluster nodes output

Next you will verify and view the cluster in Anthos dashboard.

Login and authenticate the cluster using Google Anthos dashboard

Login to the Anthos Dashboard and click *View clusters* as shown in figure 3.11.

Figure 3.11 - Anthos Dashboard

You would see the cluster – *bm-demo-cluster*. This cluster was registered to the Hub Anthos GKE Connect agent. The GKE Connect agent is installed on the pods in the *bm-demo-cluster* during installation, which periodically provides the cluster status and listens to required activity feeds from the Hub.

The *bm-demo-cluster* has a warning sign as shown in figure 3.12. This is because you are not yet logged in to the cluster..

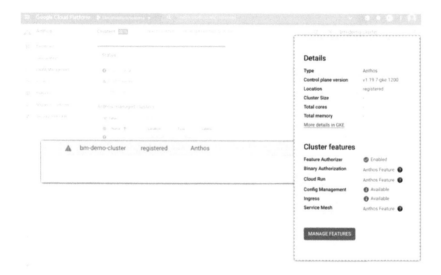

Figure 3.12 - Cluster details

Select the cluster and you will get a screen with the Login option. Click on Login and it will show four options to authenticate the cluster. You will use the token option, to authenticate the cluster and view the cluster details.

To get the access token, you will first need to create a Kubernetes service account (KSA). You will then create a cluster-admin role to allow any installation from Google Marketplace in future.

First export the kube configuration file.

```
export KUBECONFIG=~/bmctl-workspace/bm-demo-cluster/bm-demo-cluster-kubeconfig
```

Then execute the following commands to create the KSA and bind the cluster admin role.

```
KSA_NAME=ks-bm

kubectl create serviceaccount ${KSA_NAME}

kubectl create clusterrolebinding kb-cl-rb \
--clusterrole cluster-admin --serviceaccount
default:${KSA_NAME}
```

Once the role is bound, get the bearer token for the KSA, using the following command

```
SECRET_NAME=$(kubectl get serviceaccount ks-bm
-o jsonpath='{$.secrets[0].name}')
```

```
kubectl get secret ${SECRET_NAME} -o
jsonpath='{$.data.token}' | base64 --decode
```

Copy the output from the previous command and paste it in the token field on the cluster Login dialog.

You should now see the green icon next to the cluster and should be able to view the cluster details as shown in figure 3.13.

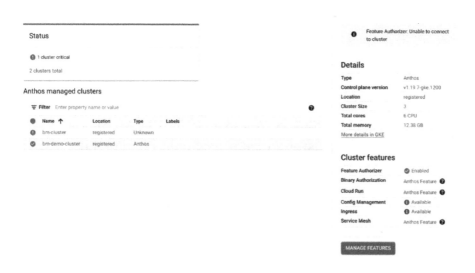

Figure 3.13 - Authenticated Cluster

Click on *More details in GKE* and you will see the bm-demo-cluster details as shown in figure 3.14.

Figure 3.14 - Authenticated Cluster Details

If you click on workloads, you can see all the workloads deployed on the cluster and status should be in green.

Name ↑	Status	Type	Pods	Namespace	Cluster
ais	OK	Deployment	1/1	anthos-identity-service	bm-demo-cluster
capi-controller-manager	OK	Deployment	1/1	capi-webhook-system	bm-demo-cluster
capi-controller-manager	OK	Deployment	1/1	capi-system	bm-demo-cluster
capi-kubeadm-bootstrap-controller-manager	OK	Deployment	1/1	capi-webhook-system	bm-demo-cluster
capi-kubeadm-bootstrap-controller-manager	OK	Deployment	1/1	capi-kubeadm-bootstrap-system	bm-demo-cluster
cert-manager	OK	Deployment	1/1	cert-manager	bm-demo-cluster
cert-manager-cainjector	OK	Deployment	1/1	cert-manager	bm-demo-cluster
cert-manager-webhook	OK	Deployment	1/1	cert-manager	bm-demo-cluster
gke-connect-agent-20210409-00-00	OK	Deployment	1/1	gke-connect	bm-demo-cluster
hello-world	OK	Deployment	1/1	default	bm-demo-cluster
istio-ingress	OK	Deployment	2/2	gke-system	bm-demo-cluster
istiod	OK	Deployment	2/2	gke-system	bm-demo-cluster

Figure 3.15 - Workload Details

If you click on Service & Ingress, you can see all the services deployed on the cluster and status should be green.

Figure 3.16 - Service - Ingress Details

Next you will deploy a sample hello world application to the cluster.

Deploy a sample application and invoke it via Load Balancer URL

In this step you will deploy a sample application to our Anthos clusters on bare metal.

Follow the steps below to deploy a sample hello world image and create a service endpoint for invocation.

1. Create the *hello-world* deployment using the pre-built Google Cloud *hello-app* container image.

```
kubectl create deployment hello-world --
image=gcr.io/google-samples/hello-app:2.0
```

2. Next view the status of deployments. You should see the hello-world deployment

```
kubectl get deployments
```

3. Expose the *hello-world* deployment using Load balancer. This will create the *hello-world* service.

```
kubectl expose deployment hello-world --
type=LoadBalancer --port=80 --target-port=8080
```

4. Next get the list of services and copy the external IP of the hello-world service

```
kubectl get services
```

```
avveen@bm-wkst:~$ kubectl get services
AME           TYPE           CLUSTER-IP     EXTERNAL-IP    PORT(S)        AGE
ello-world    LoadBalancer   10.96.14.34    10.200.0.51    80:30479/TCP   17s
ubernetes     ClusterIP      10.96.0.1      <none>         443/TCP        62m
avveen@bm-wkst:~$ 
```

Figure 3.17 - Service Details

5. Invoke the *hello-world* service using the following command

```
curl -I http://<EXTERNAL-IP>
```

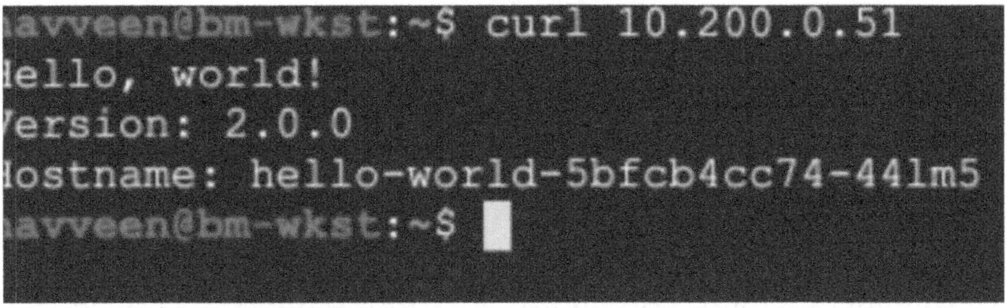

Figure 3.18 - Service Invocation Output

You should see the hello world message being printed. You have successfully deployed and tested the sample application on the Anthos bare metal cluster.

SUMMARY

In this Chapter, you went through the Google Anthos clusters on bare metal offering and looked at the installation and deployment model supported by it. You also looked at deploying a sample application on the bare metal cluster and invoked using the load balancer.

Anthos clusters on bare metal provides the flexibility to enterprises to run Anthos GKE clusters directly within their own on-premises data center, without the overhead of any virtualised environment.

Running Anthos clusters directly on your own infrastructure, gives the same unified capabilities of managing and monitoring Anthos on the cloud with improved performance, security, cost and direct control of the applications running inside your own enterprise infrastructure.

In the next chapter, you will look at implementing service management infrastructure using Anthos Service Mesh (ASM).

For detailed step by step installation guide, do checkout the YouTube video - https://www.youtube.com/playlist?list=PL42TJmsjarLcV_dSupNmgzNZbAnlJnww_ (Kindly refer to Episode 6 in the series)

CHAPTER 4 : ANTHOS SERVICE MESH

In chapter 1, we discussed how the advent of microservices created the need for dedicated service infrastructure fulfilled by Anthos Service Mesh (ASM). We briefly looked at ASM features or functions at the high level. In this chapter we will further deep dive into the features of ASM.

Later in the sections, we will use a simple use case to demonstrate basic working of ASM followed by use cases implementing advanced ASM deployment topology to show service mesh workloads in a multi cluster scenario.

ANTHOS SERVICE MESH FEATURES

ASM is backed by Istio - Google's very own open sourced service mesh initiative. It means, with ASM, you will get a fully tested and supported distribution of Istio managed by Google. ASM can be viewed as an enterprise flavour of Istio that supports and inherits all the functions and features of the open source distribution.

Let's look at some of the core features offered by ASM:

Security

- ASM by default encrypts all the mesh traffic using mutual TLS or mTLS. It also manages rotation of mTLS keys and certificates without dropping a connection.

- Provides a single root of trust through a managed multi-regional and scalable private Certificate Authority called Mesh CA for issuing mTLS certificates.

- ASM integrates with Identity Aware Proxy (IAP) to enable secure user authentication for accessing service exposed on ingress gateway. IAP can issue JWT and RCToken that can be used to authorise requests to the gateway.

- ASM user authentication offers a component called *authservice* that integrates with OIDC provider to facilitate interactive and consent based authentication through the use of RCToken

- Provides ability to audit your access to the workloads or services.

Observability

- Provides uniform observability through the use of Cloud Monitoring and Cloud Logging services.

- Provide ability to create and monitor Service Level Objectives (SLOs) that captures service performance in a given period.

- Supports integration with Prometheus to export metrics.

- Supports integration with Cloud Trace, Jaeger and Zipkin for service tracing.

Traffic Control and Networking

- Provides support for ingress gateway for traffic coming into the mesh, egress gateway for traffic leaving the mesh and east-west gateway for multi cluster service communication across networks.

- Provides support for Envoy proxies as sidecar container that intercepts traffic to and from your workloads, to provide cross cutting functionality and traffic control.

- Provides the ability to perform canary release by splitting and directing a certain portion of traffic to the new version of the service, allowing you to make gradual rollout.

Operations and Management

- Provides support for managed control plane with Google managing reliability, upgrades, scaling and security of the control plane.

- Provides support for an in-cluster control plane that is represented by Google provided *istiod* component. You will be responsible for management and operations of an in-cluster control plane.

- Allows you to manage legacy applications or services running on VMs (Compute Engines).

- Just like the canary release for services or applications, it supports canary upgrades for control plane component, allowing you to gradually roll out new revision of control plane component.

ANTHOS SERVICE MESH SAMPLE APPLICATION

In this section, we will demonstrate the capabilities of Anthos Service Mesh (ASM) through the use of a simple application. Before you proceed, make sure you have the Anthos clusters with ASM enabled. For details, on the setup, please refer to Chapter 2.

We will deploy a simple application that consists of four skeleton microservices. Each microservice does nothing but simply prints a simple statement like **Invoked service #**. The services are named *service1*, *service2*, *service3* and *service4* (These are Kubernetes service names). The *service2* will have two versions viz. v1 and v2 and therefore there will be two separate deployments of it. Later on, you will see how the request is load balanced between these two versions. The main or frontend service is *service1* that invokes *service2* and *service3*. Later you will see *service4* in action when we will demonstrate the mTLS use case.

The communication graph of the services looks like the diagram as shown in figure 4.1.

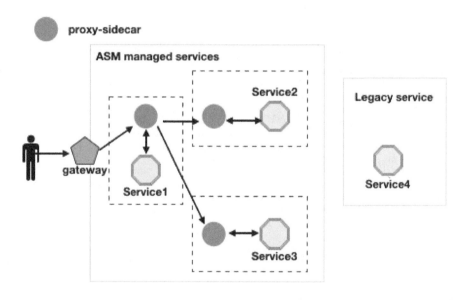

Figure 4.1 - Service Communication Graph

We will have the first three services managed under ASM i.e each of these services will have sidecar proxy container and the last service *service4* will be an isolated service, (without proxy container) not under ASM. The first three services will be part of *asm* Kubernetes namespace and the last one will be part of *legacy* namespace. To create the two namespace, use the standard *kubectl create namespace* command.

```
kubectl create namespace asm
```

```
kubectl create namespace legacy
```

The complete source code can be found at https://github.com/cloudsolutions-academy/anthos-demo-asm

In order to make these services work under the realm of ASM, you will perform the following steps:

- Enabling Sidecar Auto-injection

- Deploying the Application

- Setting up Ingress Gateway

- Testing the Application

- Enforcing mTLS Communication

- Setting Service Level Objective (SLO)

Once the application is tested, we will explore a use case to enforce mutual TLS (mTLS) for our services.

We will also look at creating service SLO and how you can use it to monitor and benchmark your service performance.

Enabling Sidecar Auto-injection

ASM provides mesh functionality through the use of sidecar containers or envoy proxies or proxy containers. The sidecar container runs alongside your primary container in the same pod. The sidecar auto-injection is performed by a mutating webhook admission controller that checks and makes sure the target namespace has the appropriate revision tag matching the control plane label. It means that the control plane component *istiod* will contain a label containing ASM revision tag that will be used to enable the automatic injection of the sidecar proxy container.

The below command will show the ASM revision tag:

```
kubectl -n istio-system get pods -l app=istiod --show-labels
```

Output:

```
istiod-asm-1120-4-dd5489f55-txhkq Running 0 16h
app=istiod,install.operator.istio.io/owning-
resource=unknown,istio.io/rev=asm-1120-4 ..
```

```
istiod-asm-1120-4-dd5489f55-z9mqq Running 0 16h
app=istiod,install.operator.istio.io/owning-
resource=unknown,istio.io/rev=asm-1120-4 ..
```

As seen from the above output, the ASM revision tag
is **asm-1120-4**.

You will now label your namespace *asm* with the above ASM
revision tag. This will spin up a sidecar or proxy container
alongside your main container as part of that namespace.

```
kubectl label namespace asm istio-injection-
  istio.io/rev=asm-1120-4 --overwrite
```

The above command will ensure that your pods as part
of **asm** namespace will now have a mesh proxy container
alongside its primary container. As you are setting this up for
the first time, you might encounter an error - **istio-injection
not found**. It is safe to ignore this error as it only means the
label *istio-injection* was not already there.

Deploying the Application

To deploy the application, you will need the Kubernetes source
config files. You can clone the source code repository using the
following path https://github.com/cloudsolutions-academy/

anthos-demo-asm. Alternatively, you can also download the source zip file and extract it in the folder of your choice.

Once the repo is cloned, navigate to each of the service*n* directory i.e *service1*, *service2*, *service3* and *service4* and build the container image and push into the container registry.

Taking the example of *service1*, you can build the image as follows.

```
gcloud builds submit --tag gcr.io/PROJECT_ID/
service1:<image-tag>
```

Replace PROJECT_ID with your Google Cloud project. The above command will build the image and push it to *gcr.io* container registry.

You will then apply the *simple-asm-app.yaml* file to the cluster in the **asm** namespace. The said file contains the first three Kubernetes services and deployments. You will apply *simple-legacy-app.yaml* file to the **legacy** namespace.

Note: Before applying the file, edit the YAML files and replace the image tag with that of yours.

```
kubectl -n asm apply -f anthos-demo-asm/k8s/simple-
asm-app.yaml
```

```
kubectl -n legacy apply -f anthos-demo-asm/k8s/
simple-legacy-app.yaml
```

You can view the deployed services by running the following command.

```
kubectl -n asm get services
```

Output:

```
NAME        TYPE        CLUSTER-IP     EXTERNAL-IP
PORT(S)              AGE
service1   ClusterIP   10.3.241.5     <none>
80/TCP,443/TCP    28h
service2   ClusterIP   10.3.248.148   <none>
80/TCP,443/TCP    28h
service3   ClusterIP   10.3.253.32    <none>
80/TCP,443/TCP    26h
```

```
kubectl -n legacy get services
```

Output:

```
service4   ClusterIP   10.3.255.30    <none>
80/TCP,443/TCP    26h
```

As you have now enabled auto-injection in the *asm* namespace, you should see a sidecar container alongside the main container in all the service pods.

```
kubectl -n asm get pods
```

Output:

```
NAME                        READY   STATUS
RESTARTS    AGE
service1-776d6db946-ftzgw    1/1    Running   0
78s
service2-v1-6f88d9bcbc-r4xlg  1/1    Running   0
78s
service3-978bff748-t7xvv     1/1    Running   0
78skubectl -n legacy get pods
service4-6c8f4ddc9-zhkhq     1/1    Running   0
78s
```

As you can see from the above output, all the pods as part of *asm* namespace have a count of two containers – one primary and another sidecar envoy proxy container. This indicates that the application services will now communicate in a mesh intercepted by the proxy container. The pod under the *legacy* namespace has only one primary application container as it is not part of ASM.

Setting up Ingress Gateway

For this application, the service named *service1* will serve as a frontend service. It means when the user accesses the application from the browser, the first service to be invoked will be *service1*. You will expose the *service1* to the Internet using the **Gateway** component of the ASM that will represent our ingress gateway. You will find the Gateway named *simple-gateway* in the *simple-app-gateway.yaml* file. The file will be part of the *network* folder in the source code.

Let's understand the **Gateway** configuration:

```
apiVersion: networking.istio.io/v1alpha3
kind: Gateway
metadata:
  name: simple-gateway
spec:
  selector:
    istio: ingressgateway
  servers:
  - port:
      number: 80
      name: http
      protocol: HTTP
    hosts:
    - "*"
```

The above Gateway configuration will expose the *service1* on port *80* as a *http* endpoint. For simplicity, you will use the value of * in the *hosts* fields that indicate match all the destination hosts. The *selector* field above specifies the ingress controller that will act as a load balancer for our frontend service.

But how does the Gateway know that it has to reach *service1*. You do this by configuring another ASM component called **VirtualService**. You will find VirtualService config defined in the same file.

Let's understand the **VirtualService** configuration:

```
apiVersion: networking.istio.io/v1alpha3
kind: VirtualService
metadata:
  name: service1-vs
spec:
  hosts:
  - "*"
  gateways:
  - simple-gateway
  http:
  - match:
    - uri:
        exact: /home
    route:
    - destination:
        host: service1
        port:
          number: 80
```

The above VirtualService named *service1-vs* binds to our *simple-gateway* Gateway and provides a *destination* as our frontend service named *service1*. It will invoke *service1* only if the URL path matches **/home**.

Apply the *simple-app-gateway.yaml* file.

```
kubectl -n asm apply -f anthos-demo-asm/network/
simple-app-gateway.yaml
```

Testing the Application

Now that we have the ingress Gateway *simple-gateway* **already** setup, the last step is to get the external IP address of this Gateway serving as a load balancer. You can get the IP by running the following command.

```
kubectl get service istio-ingressgateway -n demo-
gateway
```

Output:

```
NAME                    TYPE            CLUSTER-IP
EXTERNAL-IP    PORT(S)
AGE
 istio-ingressgateway   LoadBalancer    10.3.247.XXX
34.87.1X.XX    15021:31099/TCP,80:30987/
```

```
TCP,443:32502/TCP,15012:30716/TCP,15443:30124/TCP
61d
```

Grab the above external IP address and invoke our service using the following URL in the browser: - *http://<external-ip>/home*

You should see the following output as shown in figure 4.2. If you keep refreshing the page, you should see versions of *service2* service (as shown in figure 4.2), load balanced in round robin fashion.

Figure 4.2 - Service Invocation outputs

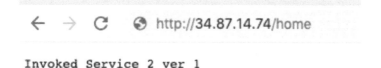

You can also view our ASM services in action in the *topology* view of the ASM dashboard from the Google Cloud console as shown in figure 4.3.

Figure 4.3 - Service Topology

If you select any of the service, say *service1*, you will see much finer details of that service like requests per second, error rate and latency as shown in figure 4.4.

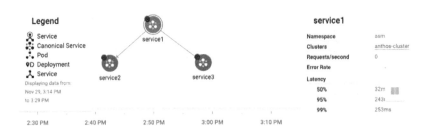

Figure 4.4 - Service Details

Please note that the *service4* does not feature in the ASM dashboard as it is not managed by ASM. We have kept *service4* to demonstrate the mTLS use case which we will cover in the next section.

Enforcing mTLS Communication

Mutual TLS or mTLS is a TLS handshake where both client and server present certificates to authenticate itself. With ASM, the mTLS feature is enabled by default and is backed by something called an authentication policy. By default, the said policy is in a **PERMISSIVE** mode. It means the service proxy can accept both plain vanilla http and mTLS traffic. If a service proxy gets a request from the AMS managed service, it automatically secures the traffic using mTLS. On the other hand, if the service proxy gets a request from the legacy service (not managed by ASM), it will continue to serve using plain http without TLS.

Let's try invoking *service3* from the legacy service *service4*

```
kubectl -n legacy exec $(kubectl get pod -n legacy
-o jsonpath={.items..metadata.name}) -- curl -s
http://service3.asm -w '%{http_code}\n'
```

```
Output:
```

```
Invoked service 3
200
```

As you can see from the above command, the legacy *service4* is able to successfully call the ASM managed service3. This happens using plain http without any TLS encryption as the default mode of policy is **PERMISSIVE**.

So how do we enforce our services to serve only using the mTLS (secured) channel? It means if a legacy service invokes the ASM service without the client certificate, it should not be allowed.

The answer lies in creating a **PeerAuthentication** policy manifest to override the authentication behavior. It's a ASM custom resource that represents the authentication policy.

Let's look at the following code:

```
## pa.yaml

apiVersion: "security.istio.io/v1beta1"
kind: "PeerAuthentication"
metadata:
  name: "namespace-policy"
  namespace: asm
spec:
```

```
mtls:
  mode: STRICT
```

The above policy will allow only mTLS traffic where the client
will have to present a certificate in order to communicate with
the service proxy (sidecar). It will apply to all workloads that
are part of *asm* namespace. The services that are part of ASM
will continue to invoke each other using mTLS with
the **STRICT** mode. Any service outside of mesh will not be
able to communicate with the ASM services. In our case, the
legacy *service4* will not be able to communicate with any of the
services in the mesh.

Let's apply the above policy manifest and again try calling ASM
managed *service3* from legacy *service4*

```
kubectl -n asm apply -f anthos-demo-asm/pa.yaml
```

Output:

```
peerauthentication.security.istio.io/mtls-strict-
policy created
```

```
kubectl -n legacy exec $(kubectl get pod -n legacy
-o jsonpath={.items..metadata.name}) -- curl -s
http://service3.asm -w'%{http_code}\n'
```

```
Output:

000
command terminated with exit code 56
```

You will now see the http code returned is **000** which indicates
the request did not go through. All the services in the mesh are
operating under **STRICT** mTLS mode and therefore the sidecar
proxy will intercept and block any plain http traffic coming
from outside of mesh.

Setting Service Level Objective (SLO)

Service Level Objectives (SLOs) are the way of measuring your
service characteristics. Some of the things you could measure
are service availability, response times, throughput or latency
and you set these indicators as measurable values as part of
your SLOs. The existence of SLOs lets you notify through an
alerting system if the service indicator value falls out of range
from the expected value. The SLOs represent the overall health
of your services that you strive to maintain. The SLOs are
devised in alignment with your end users expectations.

With ASM, you can set the service SLO using the following
Service Level Indicators (SLI)s: **Availability** and **Latency**.

Availability is the measure of time in percentage (%), your
service will successfully respond to the requests. The SLI is
measured as the ratio of sum of total good requests to the total

requests in a given period. The good request means that it responded successfully without error. For a typical web request, any response with error code that is not 5xx is termed as a good request. All 5xx response codes are system or backend errors that qualify as bad requests.

Latency is a service response time measured in milliseconds. It is a duration of request in a given period of time measured as percentiles. For example, if you have set $<=200ms$ as an acceptable response time over a period of 10 minutes, then 95th percentile means determining whether 95% of the requests responded within 200ms in a given 10 minute span.

For our use case, you will create a SLO with *Availability* as SLI and target as 97% in a given calendar day . It means our service should be available and respond successfully 97% of the time for the duration of the day.

Let's create the SLO.

Creating SLO

You will create SLO for *service1* as this is a frontend service that gets requests directly from end users via load balancer.

You can set the following objectives for *service1*.

- Request Duration: Single day

- 97% Availability – Means 97% requests must be successful

- Error Budget (100%) – Upto 3% requests can fail.

If more than 3% requests fail, the **Error Budget** starts decreasing and that indicates an unhealthy service or application not meeting the SLO. You want to make sure that your Error Budget does not fall below a certain threshold limit that you set as per your Error Budget policy.

Note, this is just a hypothetical use case to make you understand the working of SLO. In an ideal scenario, SLOs are derived in alignment with your users or benchmarked through regular observation of your application services.

Go to the ASM dashboard and click on *service1*. One the left hand panel, click on *Health*. As there are no SLOs already created, you will not see any health details about the *service1*. Click on *Create SLO* button as shown in figure 4.5.

Figure 4.5 - Create SLO

As part of SLI details, choose **Availability** as a metric and

Request-based as a method of evaluation as shown in figure 4.6.

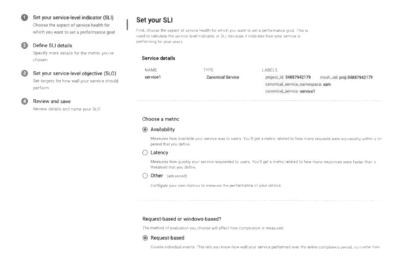

Figure 4.6 - Set SLI

For setting the SLO, select the **Compliance** period of 1 calendar day and the target **Performance** goal to be 97% as shown in figure 4.7. Click on the Create SLO button.

Figure 4.7 - Set SLO

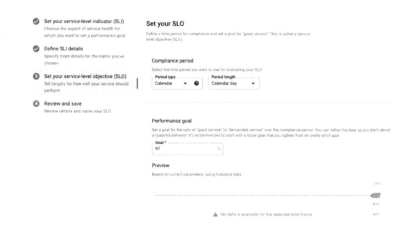

Once the SLO for *service1* is created, click on the SLO and you will see the status details that will reflect the Error Budget as 100% as shown in the figure 4.8. It means the service is healthy and so far all the requests are successfully responded to.

Figure 4.8 - Service Status Details

You will now simulate requests to *service1* using simple shell script commands. The below command will **curl** the load balancer URL invoking *service1* in a loop with a lag of 1 second and output the http response code.

```
while true;
    do curl -o /dev/null -s -w '%{http_code}\n'
http://35.198.194.178/home;
sleep 1;
done
```

The above command will execute in an infinite loop. Keep the terminal open and running.

As you know our services are skeleton services that only prints a one liner message, so you may not see any significant impact on the performance. The Error Budget will be still 100%.

You will now simulate a failure condition by deleting the *service3* from the cluster. Run the below command in a separate terminal window.

```
kubectl -n asm delete svc service3
```

You will now start seeing *503* error being printed on the first terminal where the loop is going on. This indicates an error as the *service3* is down.

Now you will see that gradually the Error Budget rate is decreasing as shown in figure 4.9 and therefore an indication that something is wrong with the application. This concludes the simulation. You can terminate the while loop command.

It is important to have a good Error Budget policy in place so that if there is a dip in the error budget, you could take some alternate action to recover your SLO in agreement with your users and key stakeholders.

Figure 4.9 - Service - Error Budget Details

Once your SLO is stabilised and becomes consistent in line with the error budget policy, you can continue on further improving your SLO and reliability of your service.

In the next section, we look at advanced deployment topology for ASM.

ADVANCED ASM TOPOLOGY

So far we looked at implementing a simple service mesh in a single cluster which is a typical setup for most applications. We will now look at implementing advanced service mesh topology spanning multiple clusters and regions. The clusters itself can contain redundant sets of services or distinct services based on the application requirement.

You have an option to setup a service mesh control plane in every Anthos cluster or you can have all the clusters communicate to one central service mesh control plane. ASM supports federated mesh where every cluster can host both service mesh control and data plane components.

Let's look at the various production deployment models supported by ASM. The deployment model provides High Availability (HA) and a decentralised approach to form a single logical mesh topology where each cluster runs its own control and data plane components.

Multi cluster service mesh (single VPC network)

In this network topology, two clusters have their own instance of ASM control plane and are part of the same Virtual Private Cloud (VPC) network. There is direct connectivity between services in the mesh across clusters. Both the clusters must be setup to trust each other. This can be achieved by exchanging secrets (certificate derived from common root CA) of the other cluster thereby enabling access to Kubernetes (GKE) API servers. In effect, cluster one will be able to access the API server and discover endpoints of the second cluster and vice versa.

The figure 4.10 shows the topology for this setup.

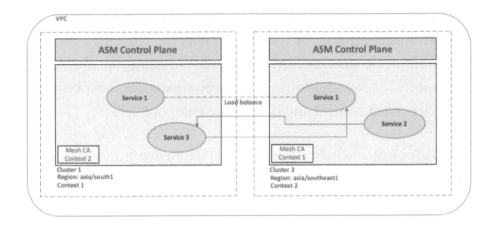

Figure 4.10 - Single VPC Multi cluster service mesh topology

As both the clusters are part of the same VPC, there is no need of routing via ingress gateway. Service endpoints in both the clusters can directly communicate with each other.

Multi cluster service mesh (different VPC networks)

In this network topology, two clusters have their own instance of ASM control plane and are set up in different VPC networks. Services in a mesh cannot communicate directly across clusters but have to make use of the gateway to route the east-west traffic. To implement this model, you have to again set up trust between clusters, as discussed in the previous section, to enable endpoints discovery across clusters. You then have to setup an ingress gateway that will allow east-west traffic in both the clusters.

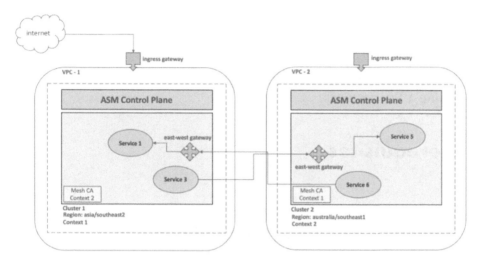

Figure 4.11 - Multi VPC Multi cluster service mesh topology

The gateway endpoint will be accessible over public internet but will expose only services with *.*local* domain. This will ensure services endpoints from both the clusters will be able to communicate via this gateway thereby enabling east-west traffic. The gateway will also ensure that only mTLS enabled services are able to communicate with each other thereby making sure that services are indeed part of the recognised clusters.

As part of this book, we will demonstrate multi-cluster ASM implementation in a single VPC network.

IMPLEMENTING MULTI CLUSTER SERVICE MESH IN A SINGLE VPC NETWORK

In this section, we will implement multi cluster ASM in a single VPC network.

Prerequisites

Before we kick start the implementation, make sure you have the following prerequisites in place.

- You have already setup a Google project with a single VPC and two regional subnets. You can opt for any available two regions to implement this use case. For our setup, we will take Mumbai as one region and Singapore as another.

- You have Anthos GKE cluster setup in both the regions along with ASM installed and enabled. To understand how to install ASM, please follow the steps outlined in Chapter 2.

- The ASM Certificate Authority (CA) used will be Mesh CA (only available for GKE clusters). This can be verified during ASM installation.

Setting the cluster context

As a first step, identify the context of each cluster. The below command will list the different cluster context.

```
kubectl config get-contexts -o name

gke_sandbox-111111_asia_south1-a_cluster-1

gke_sandbox-111111_asia_southeast1-a_cluster-2
```

The cluster context name, by default, follows a pattern: *project-id_cluster-location_cluster_name*. Assign the context name to *$ctx1* and *$ctx2* environment variables, each representing cluster one and two respectively.

```
export ctx1=gke_sandbox-111111_asia_south1-
a_cluster-1

export ctx2=gke_sandbox-111111_asia_southeast1-
a_cluster-2
```

Setting endpoint discovery between clusters

In this step you will enable each cluster to discover service endpoints of their counterpart, so that cluster one will discover service endpoints of the second cluster and vice versa.

```
istioctl x create-remote-secret --context=$ctx1 --
name=cluster-1 | \
kubectl apply -f - --context=$ctx2
```

```
istioctl x create-remote-secret --context=$ctx2 --
name=cluster-2 | \
kubectl apply -f - --context=$ctx1
```

You enable this by creating secrets for each cluster that grants access to kube API server of that cluster. Each secret is the certificate derived from the common root CA, in this case Mesh CA. You then apply the secret to the other cluster. In that way secrets are exchanged and the clusters are able to see the service endpoints of each other.

Creating sample microservices application

The application as part of this use case is a simple NodeJS application that prints the service name. Below is the sample code:

```
'use strict';
const express = require('express');

const PORT = 9000;
const HOST = '0.0.0.0';

const app = express();
app.get('/', (req, res) => {
res.send('Service 1: version 1.0\n\n');
});

app.listen(PORT, HOST);
console.log(Running on http://${HOST}:${PORT});
```

You will deploy four distinct deployments (containers) of the above application – nodeapp1 (ver 1) and nodeapp3 deployments in the first cluster and nodeapp1 (ver 2) and nodeapp2 deployments in the second cluster. The source for the application is available at https://github.com/cloudsolutions-academy/anthos-demo-asm-multicluster

Our mesh topology will look like the following as shown in figure 4.12.

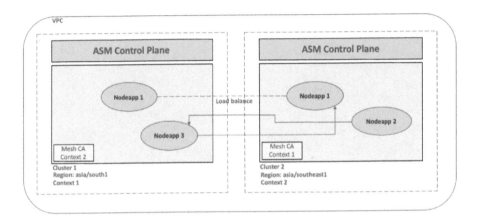

Figure 4.12 - Sample Mesh Topology

We will use *nodeapp1* service to demonstrate load balancing – where request to common *nodeapp1* service can either print 'version 1' or 'version 2'. We will also demonstrate communication between two different services i.e *nodeapp3* and *nodeapp2*. All the services will be able to communicate with each other through direct endpoint discovery. There will be no gateway routing involved as all the services are part of the same VPC.

Our Kubernetes resource deployment setup will look like the following:

Cluster Name	Kubernetes Service	Kubernetes Deployment
cluster-1	nodeapp1 ǀ ClusterIP ǀ 80:9000	nodeapp1-v1
	nodeapp3 ǀ ClusterIP ǀ 80:9000	nodeapp3
	nodeapp2 ǀ ClusterIP ǀ 80:9000	
cluster-2	nodeapp1 ǀ ClusterIP ǀ 80: 9000	nodeapp1-v2
	nodeapp2 ǀ ClusterIP ǀ 80:9000	nodeapp2
	nodeapp3 ǀ ClusterIP ǀ 80:9000	

To setup the above Kubernetes services and deployments, follow the steps below.

```
git clone https://github.com/cloudsolutions-academy/
anthos-demo-asm-multicluster
```

```
cd anthos-demo-asm-multicluster/
```

For each of the *nodeapp* folder under *microservices* folder, build the container image and push the image into the google container registry. (similar to step mentioned in *Deploying the Application* section earlier)

You will then apply the deployment and service configuration to the respective cluster as shown below, aligning with the deployment table mentioned earlier.

```
kubectl config use-context $ctx1

kubectl apply -f cluster1-deploy.yaml

kubectl config use-context $ctx2

kubectl apply -f cluster2-deploy.yaml
```

You will execute the deployments in the default namespace. Before deploying, enable auto injection of sidecars on the default namespace. For details on enabling auto-injection, refer to earlier section named *Enabling Sidecar Auto-injection*

The mesh will use Kubernetes DNS to resolve the service name with its endpoint. In order for the DNS lookup to be successful, the target services must be deployed in both the clusters even if there are no instances of the service's pod running in the client (calling) cluster. If the endpoint is not found in the calling cluster the mesh will route the request to the second cluster.

Testing service to service communication

Before you start testing service to service communication, you need to first configure the firewall to allow bidirectional communication between Pods of two clusters.

By default, when you create the GKE cluster in a VPC network, an ingress rule entry is automatically created in the Firewall, allowing all the Pods in the cluster to communicate with each other. The entry name typically starts with prefix 'gke' followed by cluster name and ends with 'all' suffix. For example, gke-cluster-1xxxxxx-all.

From the Google Cloud Console, click on *Navigation menu > VPC Network > Firewall*. You can find and edit the entry with the suffix 'all' for your cluster and add the Pod CIDR of the second cluster, as part of the *Source IP range* field. Click *Save*. Similarly, perform the same steps for the second cluster and add the Pod CIDR range of the first cluster.

Now Pods from both the clusters are allowed to communicate with each other.

To test the cross-cluster communication, you can call the *nodeapp1* service from *nodeapp3* pod.

```
kubectl config use-context $ctx1
```

```
kubectl exec -it $(kubectl get pod -l app=nodeapp3
-o jsonpath='{.items[0].metadata.name}') -- curl
http://nodeapp1/
```

Invoke this multiple times and you will see load balancing in
action. It will print output from both the versions of
service nodeapp1

```
Service1: ver 1.0
Service1: ver 2.0
```

You can also test the communication
between *nodeapp3* and *nodeapp2*. You can invoke
the *nodeapp2* service from the *nodeapp3* pod.

```
kubectl exec -it $(kubectl get pod -l app=nodeapp3
-o jsonpath='{.items[0].metadata.name}') -- curl
http://nodeapp2/
```

As you can see it is so easy and seamless to setup cross-cluster
mesh and enable communication across clusters in a single
network. In the next section, we will look at how to implement
cross-cluster mesh in two different VPC networks.

SUMMARY

In this chapter, you got the handle of the rich set of features provided by ASM backed by Istio. You learned how to create simple service mesh and understood basic traffic flow with and without mTLS. You also learned the concept of service SLO and how you can create service SLI and observe service performance using Error Budget. The chapter also looked at implementing advanced ASM topologies that involved multi cluster mesh.

In the next chapter, we will cover serverless architecture in the container world and look at implementing one of its core service - Cloud Run for Anthos.

CHAPTER 5 : CLOUD RUN FOR ANTHOS

The word *serverless* took the world by storm. Let's talk a bit about this concept called serverless. We all know serverless means running a piece of code on the cloud without worrying about the underlying infrastructure – also called 'function as a service'. This is what we call a programming model of serverless. There is another perspective or dimension to serverless and that is called managed service or managed infrastructure. The Google cloud extends the definition of serverless as being any service of which its underlying infrastructure is managed by the cloud provider to facilitate dynamic scaling and pay-per-use model. This is the **operations model** of serverless. It can be perceived as services giving you a serverless experience. Some of the examples are Cloud Storage, BigQuery, Cloud SQL or a PaaS platform like App Engine. A developer simply uses and configures the service and does not worry about how the underlying infrastructure operates on the service to keep it resilient and available.

Google Cloud introduced another such serverless platform called Cloud Run that provides a serverless experience in the world of containers. The containers can be run as HTTP workloads and they are dynamically scaled by Cloud Run without the need of writing any scaling routines. The developer simply writes the business logic and pushes it as a container and lets the platform do the rest like deploying, running and scaling the workload. The Cloud Run platform handles all of the low level routines like setting up load balancers, domain mapping, autoscaling, TLS handshaking, identity & access control, logging and monitoring.

CLOUD RUN FOR ANTHOS OVERVIEW

Cloud Run for Anthos (CRA) is a Google Cloud managed service that provides serverless experience on Anthos Google Kubernetes Engine (GKE). It allows you to configure, build, deploy and run serverless workloads on Anthos GKE and on-prem Kubernetes cluster. The said service is backed by Knative platform that offers features like scale-to-zero, autoscaling and eventing framework. CRA is a layer built on top of Knative framework with the focus on increasing productivity by improving developer experience and solving issues related to deployment, routing, scaling to name a few, in Kubernetes.

In this chapter we will cover the deployment model and architecture of CRA and later in the section demonstrate building and deploying a sample application using CRA.

Knative is an open source framework that provides serverless experience for your containers or workloads in Kubernetes. It is a layer or an abstraction over Kubernetes hiding away complexities of networking and scaling and making it easy for developers to deploy workloads. As per the official website – it solves the boring but difficult parts of deploying and managing cloud native services for you.

DEPLOYMENT MODEL

The CRA deployment model is an extension of Kubernetes and consists of Custom Resource Definition (CRD) resources in the form of Service, Configuration, Revision and Route. Let's look at the definition of each of these in the context of CRA.

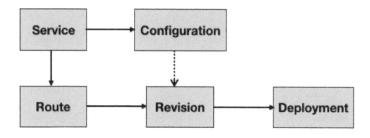

Figure 5.1 - Deployment Model for CRA

Service

In CRA, a Service represents an application workload which is exposed via an HTTP URL. The application container must be a Web application serving on a specific port. The CRA Service, by default, serves the application on port 8080 unless specified with a specific port. The service YAML is more like a stripped version of Kubernetes deployment resource.

The below is the sample CRA service YAML which looks a lot like Kubernetes resource YAML:

```
apiVersion : serving.knative.dev/v1
kind : Service
metadata :
  name : hello
spec :
  template :
    metadata :
      name : hello-v1
    spec :
      containers :
      - image : gcr.io/cloudrun/hello
```

When you look at the above code, you will see that it resembles a combination of Kubernetes Deployment and Service resource. But it is different from Kubernetes. It is

Knative in action. The value of *apiVersion* tells us that it is a Knative Serving Service with the *kind* as Service. The Service name is *hello* and the revision name is *hello-v1*. If you do not put the revision name, then it will be auto generated when deployed. When you deploy the above CRA Service, it also creates Configuration, Revision and Route.

Configuration

The Configuration reflects the current desired state of the deployment. The Configuration resource YAML looks almost like the Service but the Service acts as a container or orchestrator that manages the underlying Configuration and Routes. The Configuration simply serves as a template of your latest or the most recent Revision. The controller, based on the desired state, will create the Kubernetes deployment (also called as Revision) behind the scenes. When you deploy a Service, it creates a Configuration resource. Both Service and Configuration can be used to create Revisions.

Revision

Revisions are snapshots of Configuration. Every change to the Service or Configuration YAML under the template section will create a new revision or deployment. The Revision represents a particular version of deployment that cannot be changed. It can be a combination of container image, environment variable, resource limits or concurrency value. If you change any of these values, a new Revision is created. A Revision is associated with a Kubernetes deployment and therefore your application can be rolled back to any previous version or do things like splitting traffic between multiple revisions (Canary) or gradually rolling out a revision (Blue-Green). Revisions can be tagged if you want it to be exposed with a different URL than the one generated.

Route

The Route represents the URL or the endpoint to invoke the CRA Service. It's an incoming HTTP request directed to a specific Revision. The route is automatically created when you create a CRA Service or Configuration. If you happen to redeploy your Service, the route will automatically point to the new Revision. When you delete the Service, the Route is automatically removed. The Route can also be used to specify the traffic behaviour for your revisions or configurations. You could specify what percentage of traffic to be routed to a particular revision or configuration.

ARCHITECTURE COMPONENTS

When you setup a GKE cluster with Cloud Run for Anthos, it will create two significant namespaces viz. *knative-serving* and *knative-eventing*. The *knative-serving* namespace serves the components that aids in dynamic scaling of your containers also scale down to zero based on the request load. The *knative-eventing* namespace serves the Eventing framework where CRA service is glued with other external sources or systems to handle and respond to events typically by way of autoscaling. For example, you may have a pipeline formed where data is pushed to Cloud Storage bucket triggering an event causing the CRA service to handle and process the same.

The book will focus on core components as part of *knative-serving* namespace from the architecture standpoint.

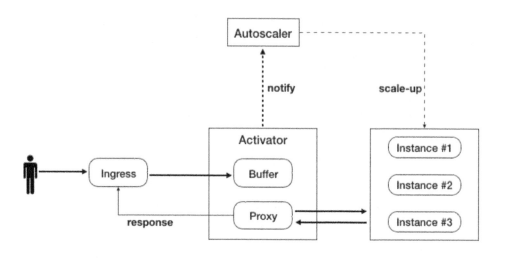

Figure 5.2 - Architecture Components for CRA

The *knative-serving* namespace serves the following components:

Autoscaler

The Autoscaler makes scaling decisions based on the number of requests and accordingly performs the scaling of instances. It checks for the request load and accordingly determines the number of instances to scale. The Autoscaler component has to make a balanced decision between the number of requests and the pods or instances to scale. It plays a role of control plane component more like a control loop to ensure that it catches up with the ongoing demand load. It will scale down to zero if there are no requests in the pipeline. Scaling down to zero is ideal but it can cause problem of cold start. When there are no instances, the first instance could take a long time to start and may throw unexpected errors to the client application. In such a situation, the Activator component comes in handy – which we will discuss next.

Activator

When there are no active application instances or pods i.e. the instances are scaled down to zero, then the client requests are directed to an Activator component. It is a component that mediates when there are no application instances to serve the requests. In such a situation, the Activator will put the request into a buffer and notify Autoscaler to start scaling the instances. Depending on the number of requests buffered, the Autoscaler makes a scaling decision and starts scaling the instances. Once there are enough instances to serve the requests, the Activator will remove itself from the data path and the ingress will directly route the requests to application instances. The Activator also plays a role when there is a sudden spike in the requests and there are not enough instances to handle the spike or load. It will ensure that Autoscaler catches up with the load before the requests are directly routed to the serving instances.

Controller

The Controller component is based on Kubernetes control loop architecture. It constantly watches the deployment resources for any state changes and updates the cluster with the desired state. It embodies a collection of processes that manages mainline deployment resources viz. Service, Configuration, Revision and Route – fulfilling or applying its desired state. It also manages low-level tasks that address how the networking works and also performs memory management through garbage collection.

Webhook

This component is modelled around Kubernetes based admission webhooks. The webhook works more like an interceptor that acts on CRA resources like Service, Configuration and Routes, before and after it is admitted or persisted. Some of the things the webhook handles are:

- Override the configuration details like timeout parameter, or concurrency limits

- Modifying or updating routing paths

- Validating the configuration details

- Embedding digest to the partial image or image with no specific tags

CREATE AND DEPLOY A SERVICE WITH CLOUD RUN FOR ANTHOS

In this section, we will demonstrate how to create and deploy a service with CRA.

This section assumes you already have Anthos setup created with GKE cluster with ASM enabled.

Install Cloud Run for Anthos on Anthos GKE cluster

To install Cloud Run, you need to enable CRA service in your Anthos environment.

The following command enables CRA service on your project

```
gcloud container hub cloudrun enable --
project=PROJECT_ID
```

Replace PROJECT_ID with your Google Cloud project.

(For more details on setting up Anthos, refer to the Chapter 2 - Anthos Installation)

For this use case, we will assume the Anthos cluster name to be *cluster-1* and the cluster location as *asia-southeast1-a* zone. You should of course follow the cluster name and location that you have created. The following command sets the default values for cluster and cluster location and sets the target platform to *gke*.

```
gcloud config set run/cluster cluster-1

gcloud config set run/cluster_location asia-
southeast1-a

gcloud config set run/platform gke
```

Setting default values for your cluster can be handy as you then need not specify it when running any CRA commands.

Next, enable CRA on your cluster by running the following command.

```
gcloud container hub cloudrun apply —gke-cluster
asia-southeast1-a/cluster-1
```

Output:
```
kubeconfig entry generated for cluster-1.
Added CloudRun CR
```

In the next section, you will develop and deploy a simple microservice application using CRA.

Developing a Service

You will create a simple service named *nodeapp* that will simply print the message **This is a simple service**. You will use Node.js to write the service and build it into Docker container. The container image will be pushed to Google Cloud Registry (gcr.io).

Below is the Node.js code that represents our service:

```
'use strict';
const express = require('express');
const PORT = 9000;
const HOST = '0.0.0.0';

const app = express();
app.get('/', (req, res) => {
  res.send('This is a simple service \n\n');
});
```

```
app.listen(PORT, HOST);
console.log(`Running on http://${HOST}:${PORT}`);
```

The above code uses express module to setup a small web runtime listening on port *9000*. You have to make sure the service is stateless and not writing anything to local persistent storage. You will have to write a Dockerfile that will be used to build the code into a container.

The below is the content of the Dockerfile:

```
FROM node:14

# Create app directory
WORKDIR /usr/src/app

# Install app dependencies
COPY package*.json ./

RUN npm install

# Bundle app source
COPY . .

CMD [ "node", "server.js" ]
```

Download the source code from https://github.com/cloudsolutions-academy/anthos-demo-cloud-run and change directory to anthos-demo-cloud-run folder.

You can build the code using Google Cloud Build service.

```
gcloud builds submit --tag=gcr.io/$GOOGLE_PROJECT/
nodeapp
```

The above command will build the application code into container image and push it to container registry (gcr.io)

Deploying the Service

In the context of CRA, the service represents application workload. The application must be backed by a container image already stored in a container registry. When you deploy a serverless service in CRA, it creates a revision which are immutable artifacts. A service can have more than one revision. There are several ways in which you can deploy a service with CRA. You could use the cloud console, write a service resource YAML or directly deploy using the command line. The below command deploys our service named *nodeapp* in the default *anthos* namespace:

```
gcloud run deploy nodeapp --image gcr.io/
<project_id>/nodeapp --cluster cluster-1 --cluster-
location asia-southeast1-a --port 9000
```

You should see a similar output.

```
✓ Deploying new service... Done.
  ✓ Creating Revision...
  ✓ Routing traffic...
Done.
Service [nodeapp] revision [nodeapp-00001-rag] has
been deployed and is serving 100 percent of traffic.
Service URL: http://nodeapp.default.example.com
```

As you can see it is so easy and simple to deploy a service and run it as a workload. All you need is the name of the service and the URL of the container image. The cluster name and location is not needed if you have already specified cloud run default cluster settings as part of configuration. The port number is required if the service is running on the port other than 8080.

You do not have to deal with Kubernetes resources like Deployments or Service or for that matter, even Ingress. The CRA service abstracts away the Kubernetes world for you. By default, it deploys the service in *anthos* namespace, so make sure you have already created the said namespace before deploying the service. If you want to deploy to some other custom namespace then specify it using *–namespace* option.

When you deploy a service it is automatically assigned *example.com* domain. The *example.com* is just an abstract host that does not serve as a load balancer or a proper

DNS-mapped entity and therefore the ingress request to this service domain will fail. You will have to use a custom domain to appropriately invoke the service using the domain name. For now, you can use Istio based ingress external IP to invoke the service – we will see this in the next section.

Viewing and Accessing the Service

You can view the the deployed services using the following command:

```
gcloud run services list
```

Output:

```
For cluster [cluster-1] in [asia-southeast1-a]:
SERVICE NAMESPACE URL LAST DEPLOYED BY LAST DEPLOYED
AT
nodeapp anthos http://nodeapp.anthos.example.com
developer@xxx.com 2021-08-20T13:03:22Z
```

The above output displays the service name, namespace and the service endpoint. The endpoint is in the format *http:// <service>.<namespace>.example.com* The service endpoint with *example.com* domain, as mentioned earlier, cannot be accessed directly as it is not mapped to DNS record. You can call the service using Istio ingress gateway. In order to do that, you will have to get the IP address and port of the Istio ingress service called *istio-ingressgateway*. The *istio-ingressgateway* service will serve as a load balancer for external traffic.

The following command will give you the ingress load balancer IP. You can note down the external IP of the *istio-ingressgateway* service which will be of type **LoadBalancer**. You will find the *istio-ingressgateway* service in *istio-system* namespace for older ASM versions. The new version of ASM will not contain *istio-ingressgateway* service and have to be separately deployed in the namespace of your choice. For details, you can refer to ASM installation in Chapter 2.

```
kubectl -n demo-gateway get svc
```

Output:

```
NAME                    TYPE            CLUSTER-IP
EXTERNAL-IP     PORT(S)
AGE
 istio-ingressgateway   LoadBalancer    10.16.12.129
34.135.xx.xx    15021:31380/TCP,80:31297/
TCP,443:32200/TCP    57s
```

You can invoke the *nodeapp* service by giving the following command:

```
curl -H "Host: nodeapp.default.example.com" http://
[CLUSTER-EXTERNAL-IP]
```

Output:

```
This is a simple service
```

The service that you just invoked is ultimately backed by Kubernetes pod. The pods will be active as far as the service revision is active. If the service is not invoked or accessed for more than 5 minutes, the CRA will automatically scale down the pods to zero.

You can also view the service invocation details in *Anthos Dashboard -> Cloud Run for Anthos*. Click on nodeapp and you would find service metrics details as shown in figure 5.3 and an option to create alerting policy based on your requirements.

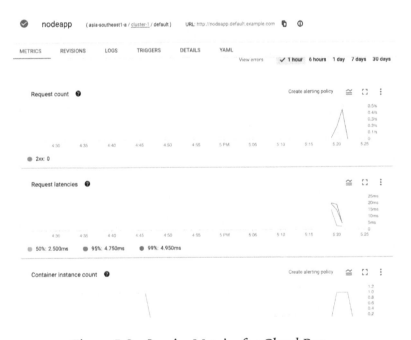

Figure 5.3 : Service Metrics for Cloud Run

You can also view logs, create triggers (i.e respond to events) and revisions for your cloud run service.

In the next section, you will look at how to update the service.

Updating the Service

When you create or update a CRA service, it creates a revision which is a versioned immutable workload that you access.

Let's look at the service YAML.

```
apiVersion: serving.knative.dev/v1
kind: Service
metadata:
  name: nodeapp
  namespace: anthos
spec:
  template:
    metadata:
      name: nodeapp-00003-bap
    spec:
      containerConcurrency: 0
      containers:
      - image: gcr.io/anthos-book-322415/nodeapp
        name: user-container
        ports:
        - containerPort: 9000
```

```
        protocol: TCP
```

The service revision name is *nodeapp-00003-bap*. Any updates made under *template->spec* section, will create another revision of the service.

The below command will list the revisions for your service:

```
gcloud run revisions list
```

Output:

```
For cluster [cluster-1] in [asia-southeast1-a]:
REVISION              ACTIVE  SERVICE  DEPLOYED
DEPLOYED BY
nodeapp-00003-bap             nodeapp  2021-08-20
13:03:16 UTC  developer@xxx.com
```

For now you have only one revision for our *nodeapp* service. Let's update the service to add an environment variable.

The below command updates the service to add an environment variable.

```
gcloud run services update nodeapp --set-env-
vars=ENV=dev
```

Now if you list the service revisions, there will be two of them.

```
For cluster [cluster-1] in [asia-southeast1-a]:
   REVISION              ACTIVE  SERVICE  DEPLOYED
DEPLOYED BY
   nodeapp-00004-voq  yes       nodeapp  2021-08-22
08:55:55 UTC  developer@xxx.com
   nodeapp-00003-bap            nodeapp  2021-08-20
13:03:16 UTC  developer@xxx.com
```

The latest one will be the active revision having our new environment variable. The service revisions allow you to roll back to the previous version or any known good version. Now when you observe the pods in the *anthos* namespace, you should see the pod associated to the latest service revision. The pod associated to the previous revision is terminated as there are no requests to it for the last 1 minute. When you invoke the service, it will automatically point to the latest revision.

Scaling the Service

With CRA, you can explicitly set the service scaling limits using the command line options *–min-instances* and *–max-instances*. If you are working with YAML, then the annotations *autoscaling.knative.dev/maxScale* and *autoscaling.knative.dev/minScale* can be used.

Let's understand these scaling options:

minScale

When there are no requests to the serving application, the CRA by default will scale down the services (pods) to zero. This could seem an obvious choice as far as autoscaling is concerned, but their arises the problem of cold start. It is the wait time or a transition time for service to scale from zero to one. When your service is scaled to zero, a request to that service will scale the pod from zero to few to handle the request. The time it takes to scale from zero to n is the cold start latency. As the cold start latency can give you undesirable effects, it is recommended to set the minimum service replica at the start.

The following command can be used to set the minimum service replica:

```
gcloud run services update nodeapp --min-instances 2
```

The above command will make sure that there will always be at least 2 replicas of service pods running.

maxScale

The CRA dynamically scales your services as per the request load. There is no upper scaling limit by default. This may not be desirable as it could potentially use all your compute resources available on the nodes. In order to control the resource usage, you can set the maximum scaling limit for your service.

The following command can be used to set the maximum number of replica:

```
gcloud run services update nodeapp --max-instances 7
```

The above command will make sure that the CRA autoscaler can scale your service pods to max 7 replicas.

As you see it is important to observe your autoscaling details and accordingly set minimum and maximum limits for your service replicas.

SUMMARY

In this chapter, you learned the basics of Google Cloud Run for Anthos service and how it helps dynamically scale your application in the world of GKE. You learned the importance of core CRD resources viz. Service, Configuration, Revision and Route as part of deployment model. The chapter also walked you through architecture building blocks as part of Knative serving. Finally, you learned how to develop and deploy a simple CRA service.

In the next chapter, we will cover how you can manage configurations across clusters using one of the core service - Anthos Config Management

CHAPTER 6 : ANTHOS CONFIG MANAGEMENT

Enterprises today are seeing proliferation of clusters in their environment and one of the biggest challenges they face is that of managing the configurations and deployments across these clusters. Anthos Config Management (ACM) is a core service in the Anthos ecosystem that provides the unified approach to configuration and deployment management in a hybrid or multi cluster environment. It enables deployment and security operators to define a common set of configurations and policies that can be applied consistently across all the clusters in a multi-cluster or hybrid environment.

In chapter 1, we had gone through the architecture and key components of ACM. In this chapter we will setup ACM and deploy a simple application that will demonstrate the core ACM functionality - Config Sync. We will also cover how to enforce a governance based policy using ACM Policy Controller.

INSTALL GOOGLE ANTHOS CONFIG MANAGEMENT

In this section, you will setup ACM using Google Cloud Console and later deploy a simple application.

Note: In Chapter 2, we described how to setup and configure ACM using command line (CLI). If you have already enabled ACM using CLI, then you can skip this section.

This setup assumes you already have Anthos clusters installed in your environment. If you do not have one already installed then you can refer to *Chapter 2 - Anthos Installation* or *Chapter 3 - Anthos Clusters on Bare Meta* for installation details.

Login to Google Cloud Console and using the navigation menu, navigate to *Anthos > Config Management*. Click on the *New Setup* button. On the next screen, select the registered cluster required for Config Management as shown in figure 6.1 and click the *Complete* button.

Figure 6.1 - Enable ACM

Once you click on the *Complete* button, it will take some time while it installs ACM components viz. Config Sync, Config Connector, Policy Controller and Hierarchy Controller on your cluster. For more details on ACM architecture and components refer to *Chapter 1 - Anthos in a Nutshell*. To verify if ACM is installed, click on *Clusters* from the left panel, select your cluster, click on *Manage Features* button on the right side panel and you should see the Config Management status as enabled as shown in figure 6.2.

Click on the *Details* action link and you will see the option to disable Config Management.

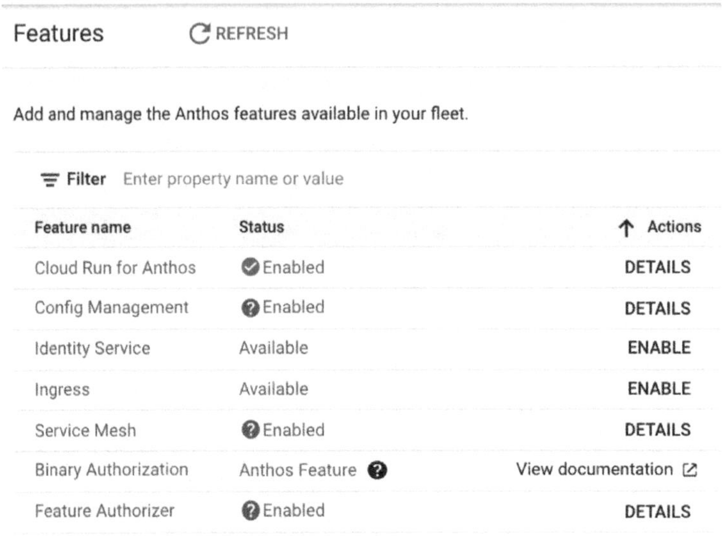

Figure 6.2 - Anthos Features

Going ahead, you will configure Config Sync to provide read only access to our *cloudsolutions-academy/anthos-acm* Git repository where all configurations are stored. The Config Sync agent will read the configs and apply them to your clusters.

In the next section, we will go over the Git repository structure that contains all the configuration.

GIT REPOSITORY FOR ANTHOS CONFIG MANAGEMENT

In this section, you will understand the source Git repository and its content.

Navigate to the Git repository of cloud solutions academy at
https://github.com/cloudsolutions-academy/anthos-acm. The
config repository is a structured repository. It consists of a
cluster, namespace and *system* directory.

```
anthos-acm/
├── cluster
├── namespaces
│    └── test
└── system
```

In Chapter 2, we discussed ACM configuration using
structured repo and walked through the content of each
directory in the structure. To recap, the *cluster* directory
contains configurations that are meant to be applied at the
cluster level (cluster-scoped objects) , the *namespace* directory
contains namespaces and configs that needs to be created and
managed by ACM in that namespace and *system* directory
contains repo config and version details. You will later see how
the Config Sync agent automatically applies the configs to our
cluster.

Click on the *cluster* directory, you will see a configuration file
pod-reader.yaml. This is a cluster role with a view only access to
pods.

```
apiVersion: rbac.authorization.k8s.io/v1
kind: ClusterRole
metadata:
```

```
  name: pod-reader
rules:
- apiGroups: [""]
  resources: ["pods"]
  verbs: ["get", "watch", "list"]
```

Next click on *namespaces* directory and you will see a *test* sub-directory. The *test* sub-directory contains *namespace.yaml* config file, which basically defines a namespace by the name as *test*. You will also see a config file named *test-pod-reader.yaml* in the *test* sub-directory.

```
apiVersion: rbac.authorization.k8s.io/v1
kind: RoleBinding
metadata:
  name: test-pod-reader
  namespace: test
subjects:
- kind: ServiceAccount
  name: default
  namespace: test
roleRef:
  kind: ClusterRole
  name: pod-reader
  apiGroup: rbac.authorization.k8s.io
```

The said config file is a *RoleBinding* that will allow the default service account of the pod in the *test* namespace to view all the pods in that namespace. It will not allow to view pods in other namespaces.

The *test* namespace will be automatically created and the configs automatically applied once the repository is synced by the ACM Config Sync agent.

Next navigate to the *system* directory. The *system* directory contains the mandated *repo.yaml* file containing the repository version and details. This directory is used by the Config Sync operator.

```
anthos-acm/system/
├── README.md
└── repo.yaml
```

In the next section, add this repository as part of configuration from the ACM dashboard.

CONFIGURE CLUSTER FOR ANTHOS CONFIG MANAGEMENT

Now that our repo structure is ready, let's configure the cluster to grant the Config Sync agent read access to the repo.

Login to *Anthos dashboard -> Config Management*. Select your cluster and click *Edit*. Select *Config Sync* from the left hand panel.

In the *Repository* field, select *Custom*.

In the **URL** field, provide the path to the Cloud Solution Academy repository - *https://github.com/cloudsolutions-academy/anthos-acm* as shown in figure 43.

For **Authentication Type** select *None*, as our repository does not require any credentials for read access.

In the **Branch** field, provide the name as *main* (we have only one branch). For the **Source format** select *hierarchy* as we are using structured repository format.

The figure 6.3 shows the configuration.

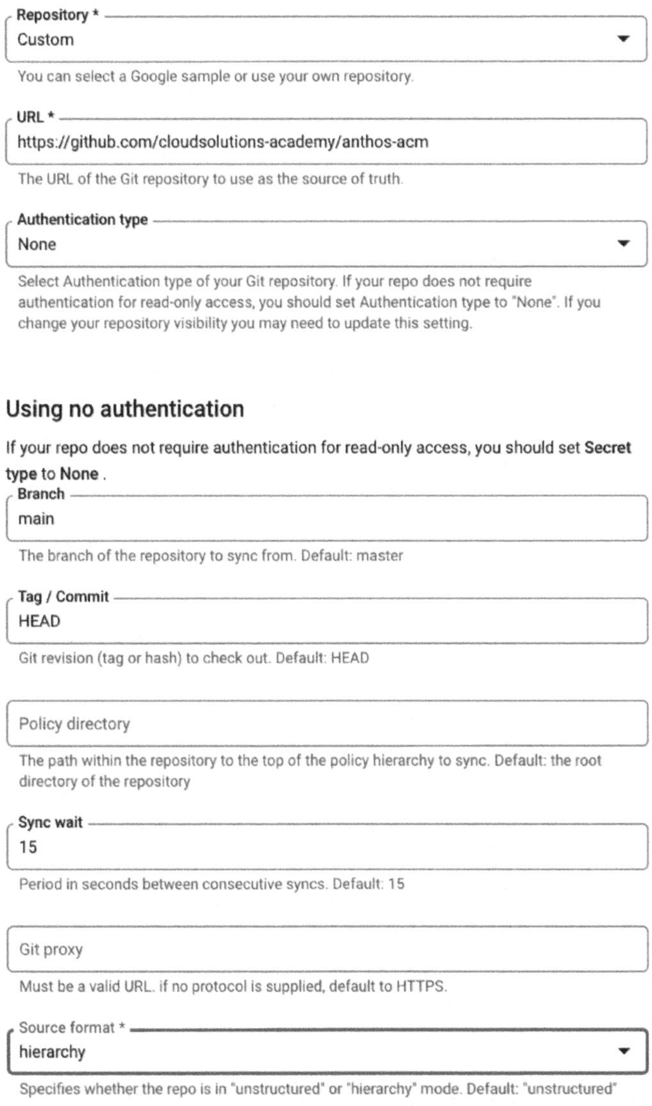

Repository *

Custom ▼

You can select a Google sample or use your own repository.

URL *

https://github.com/cloudsolutions-academy/anthos-acm

The URL of the Git repository to use as the source of truth.

Authentication type

None ▼

Select Authentication type of your Git repository. If your repo does not require authentication for read-only access, you should set Authentication type to "None". If you change your repository visibility you may need to update this setting.

Using no authentication

If your repo does not require authentication for read-only access, you should set **Secret type** to **None** .

Branch

main

The branch of the repository to sync from. Default: master

Tag / Commit

HEAD

Git revision (tag or hash) to check out. Default: HEAD

Policy directory

The path within the repository to the top of the policy hierarchy to sync. Default: the root directory of the repository

Sync wait

15

Period in seconds between consecutive syncs. Default: 15

Git proxy

Must be a valid URL. if no protocol is supplied, default to HTTPS.

Source format *

hierarchy ▼

Specifies whether the repo is in "unstructured" or "hierarchy" mode. Default: "unstructured"

Figure 6.3 : Config Sync configuration

Click *Complete*. It will take a couple of minutes to sync the repository and create the required objects in your Anthos cluster.

You should now see your cluster status as *Synced,* indicating that it successfully synced the config files i.e pulled the latest config files from the repo and applied it to the cluster.

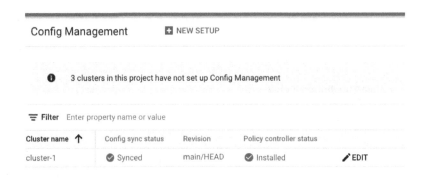

Config Management   ➕ NEW SETUP

ℹ   3 clusters in this project have not set up Config Management

≡ **Filter**   Enter property name or value

Cluster name ↑	Config sync status	Revision	Policy controller status	
cluster-1	✅ Synced	main/HEAD	✅ Installed	✏ EDIT

Figure 6.4: Sync status

If you get an error during synchronisation, you can inspect the logs by connecting to your Anthos cluster and executing the *kubectl logs* command for the *config-management-system* component as shown below.

Figure 6.5: Sync logs

As you see, all logs are clean and synchronisation was successful.

There is another optional tool called *nomos,* which can also be used to debug problems with **Config Sync** component.

To download *nomos* for Linux, run the following command and make the downloaded file executable.

```
gsutil cp gs://config-management-release/released/
latest/linux_amd64/nomos nomos
```

```
chmod +x /path/to/nomos
```

To check the synchronisation status, run `nomos status` command and you should see the repository is successfully synced as shown in figure 6.6.

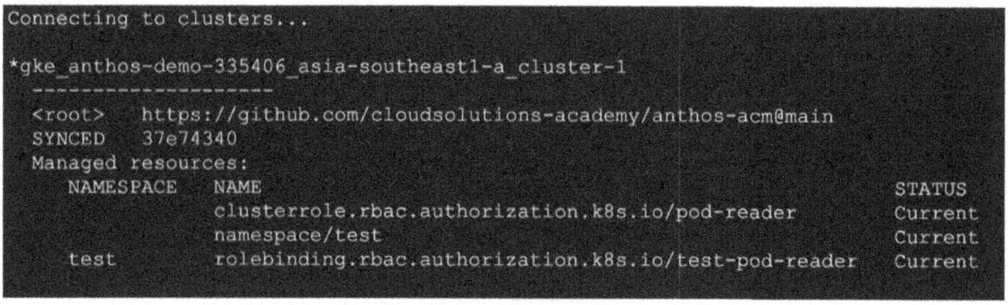

Figure 6.6: Nomos sync status

Now let's view the *test* namespace automatically created by the Config Sync agent. Run the following command

```
kubectl get ns -l "app.kubernetes.io/managed-
by=configmanagement.gke.io"
```

Output
```
NAME    STATUS    AGE
test    Active    30m
```

The latest configs as part of `cluster/` and `namespaces/test/` repo directories are also applied automatically to the cluster. You can see below *pod-reader* cluster role and *test-pod-reader* role binding configs.

```
kubectl get clusterrole pod-reader
```

Output

```
NAME          CREATED AT
pod-reader    2021-12-18T13:28:59Z
```

```
kubectl -n test get rolebinding
```

Output

```
NAME               ROLE                     AGE
test-pod-reader    ClusterRole/pod-reader   16h
```

You can try to delete the *test* namespace and you should receive an error as shown below.

```
kubectl delete namespace test
```

Output
```
error: You must be logged in to the server
(admission webhook "v1.admission-
webhook.configsync.gke.io" denied the request: User
is not authorized to delete managed resource
"_namespace_test")
```

The admission webhook component that is installed as part of ACM ensures you can't modify the managed objects directly.

In the next section, you will look at how to enforce a governance policy using ACM Policy Controller.

ENFORCING POLICY USING ANTHOS CONFIG MANAGEMENT'S POLICY CONTROLLER

ACM Policy Controller is based on Open Policy Agent (OPA) Gatekeeper project and contains a library of predefined policies that can be used to guard your cluster against any compliance or security violation. The policy you write acts as a guardrail that enforces a rule that determines whether the target resource should be admitted into the cluster or not. It acts as an admission controller webhook that integrates with Kubernetes API server to validate the objects as they are admitted to the cluster. The guardrail can also be used to audit objects for any security loophole.

The ACM Policy Controller uses the OPA Gatekeeper project which models a constraint based framework. The said framework has three main components:

- Constraint

- Rego

- Constraint template

Constraint

A constraint represents a policy. Constraints are objects that let you specify what field or values, in manifest file, are not allowed or denied as part of the policy. If there is no constraint defined, it means the manifest or resource specification is implicitly allowed to be processed by the Kubernetes API server thereby admitting it into the cluster. A constraint enforces validation. The ACM Policy Controller comes with a set of predefined constraints as part of the constraint library. The library has a lot of useful policies that can be used with your cluster to create a standard governance model.

Rego

Policy is written in a OPA based query language called Rego. Rego can easily reference nested documents and therefore is more suitable with JSON and YAML format files. The queries you write in Rego are more like assertions on data stored in OPA. The language itself is declarative allowing you to write simple statements like queries that simply return values. A rego language is used in the constraint template which we will see in the next section.

Constraint template

It is a policy template that can be made portable and reusable. It is in effect a Custom Resource Definition (CRD) that allows you to templatize the behaviour of the policy using typed parameters and custom logic. The custom logic is written in Rego query language, which along with parameters and error messages defines your policy. Once the template is created, it can be invoked by using a constraint. It is in the constraint object that you pass the actual values, to be applied to a policy, to the template parameters.

Enforcing a Sample Policy

Let us see each of the above components in action. You will create a policy that will allow only Google container registry as the source for your container images. If the Kubernetes deployment contains an image from a non-Google container registry then it should not be allowed to create the deployments.

Creating Constraint template

The following constraint template will allow only those container image repos whose name matches a value provided as part of the constraint (you will see later how to create a constraint).

```
## constraint-template.yaml

apiVersion: templates.gatekeeper.sh/v1beta1
kind: ConstraintTemplate
metadata:
  name: k8svalidimagerepos
spec:
  crd:
    spec:
```

```yaml
    names:
      kind: K8sValidImageRepos
    validation:
      # Schema for the `parameters` field
      openAPIV3Schema:
        properties:
          repos:
            type: array
            items:
              type: string
  targets:
    - target: admission.k8s.gatekeeper.sh
      rego: |
        package k8svalidimagerepos

        violation[{"msg": msg}] {
          container :=
input.review.object.spec.template.spec.containers[_]
          satisfied := [good | repo =
input.parameters.repos[_] ; good =
startswith(container.image, repo)]
          not any(satisfied)
          msg := sprintf("container <%v> has an
invalid image repo <%v>, allowed repos are %v",
[container.name, container.image,
input.parameters.repos])
        }
```

There are three significant parts to observe from the above code. The first is the name of the resource *k8svalidimagerepos* that you will reference later (from the constraint). The second is the schema for the input parameter as part of the *validation* field. In our case, the parameter is the list of repos specified as an array of strings. You will pass the actual name of the container image repo from the constraint resource. The third part is the rego code as part of the *target* field. It checks if the deployment container image name provided as an input is valid or not. If not then it will indicate a violation of policy and return with an error message.

You will now create the constraint that will refer to the above template and pass the container image repo name as a parameter to the template.

Creating Constraint

The constraint is a way of enforcing a policy. The below constraint will pass the container image repo name as an input that will be used as an image source.

```
## contraint.yaml

apiVersion: constraints.gatekeeper.sh/v1beta1
kind: K8sValidImageRepos
metadata:
  name: allowed-repo-gcr
```

```
spec:
  match:
    kinds:
      - apiGroups: ["*"]
        kinds: ["Deployment"]
    namespaces:
      - "staging"
  parameters:
    repos:
      - "gcr"
```

Let's observe the above code carefully. The
constraint *kind K8sValidImageRepos* is the same as the template
name. This indicates that the above policy uses
the *k8svalidimagerepos* constraint template. The *spec* field
contains the matching resource on which this policy will be
applied. The above code applies the policy to **Deployments** as
part of *staging* namespace. The parameters field is the input you
provide that matches the constraint template schema that you
defined earlier. In this case, it is the name(s) of the container
image repo you want to allow. For this example, you will allow
only the Google container registries as the image source and it
starts with the prefix *gcr*.

To sum up, the above constraint is a policy in effect that only
allows image registries with prefix as *gcr* defined in
the deployment as part of *staging* namespace. The constraint
makes use of *k8svalidimagerepos* constraint template to enforce
this policy.

Testing the Policy

Download (or clone) the source code from *https://github.com/cloudsolutions-academy/anthos-demo-acm-policy* and change directory to *anthos-demo-acm-policy* folder.

Apply the constraint template and the constraint manifest files to the Anthos cluster

```
kubectl apply -f constraint-template.yaml
```

```
kubectl apply -f constraint.yaml
```

Once the template and constraint resources are created, you will test the policy by creating a sample Deployment in the *staging* namespace.

Create the sample Deployment manifest file that will fetch the container image from the docker hub. As our policy only allows image from Google container repo prefixed with *gcr*, the Deployment creation should fail.

```
## nodeapp-deploy.yaml

apiVersion: apps/v1
kind: Deployment
```

```
metadata:
  name: nodeapp
  namespace: staging
  labels:
    app: nodeapp
spec:
  replicas: 1
  selector:
    matchLabels:
      app: nodeapp
  template:
    metadata:
      labels:
        app: nodeapp
    spec:
      containers:
      - name: nodeapp
        image: registry.docker.hub.com/nodeapp
        ports:
        - containerPort: 9000
```

The above deployment nodeapp tries to fetch the image from the docker hub.

First create the staging namespace and then create the deployment.

```
kubectl create namespace staging
```

```
kubectl -n staging apply -f nodeapp-deploy.yaml
```

Output:

```
Error from server ([allowed-repo-gcr] container
<nodeapp> has an invalid image repo
<registry.docker.hub.com/nodeapp>, allowed repos are
["gcr"]): error when creating "nodeapp-deploy.yaml":
admission webhook "validation.gatekeeper.sh" denied
the request: [allowed-repo-gcr] container <nodeapp>
has an invalid image repo <registry.docker.hub.com/
nodeapp>, allowed repos are ["gcr"]
```

The above fails to create the deployment as the container image source is the docker hub. It will display the error message we programmed as part of our Rego code earlier.

As you can see, the policy and governance are important security aspects that are addressed by ACM's Policy Controller through OPA Gatekeeper framework. It allows you to write user defined policies that keeps the Kubernetes clusters compliant as per the policy.

SUMMARY

In this chapter, you learned how to setup and configure ACM using a hierarchical (structured) source repository. You learned the significance of each directory in the structured repo. You also looked at deploying a simple application and configuring Config Sync to manage and sync the source configs between repo and the cluster. The chapter also focused on creating and enforcing a governance based policy that can help in setting up regulation and compliance models for your cluster.

In the next chapter, you will look at how you can extend your GKE environment to the AWS cluster.

CHAPTER 7 : ANTHOS ON AWS

Enterprises today have workloads spread around the world in multiple regions and therefore there are very high chances one single cloud provider might not fulfil all the requirements. Multi cloud strategy is inevitable. With the growing options in the public cloud provider space, most enterprises today have their workloads deployed within two or more cloud providers. This could be to avoid cloud vendor lock-in or want to leverage a specific service feature provided by another cloud vendor.

Some of the key business drivers in adopting multi-cloud strategy are:

- **Cost optimisation:** You may want to compare costs of services offered by different cloud vendors and choose the right mix or blend that gives you the most optimised solution, both from cost and performance perspective.

- **Adopting multiple cloud services:** Enterprise, today, often wants to go agile and avoid vendor lock-in by trying out different products or services offered by cloud providers. One single cloud provider might not fulfil all the requirements.

- **Security Risks:** Putting all the workloads or data within a single cloud provider can put you at the risk of a single point of failure. It is always a good idea to spread your workloads among multiple cloud vendors and reduce the attack surface.

- **Data Governance:** Data locality is the key for data governance. Due to legal and compliance requirements, you may not want to move your data out of a particular region. Such a situation may call for the need to optimise your data migration and storage costs by choosing the right mix of cloud providers in that region.

- **Application Modernisation:** Cloud providers today offer various tools that can help modernise the workloads deployed in the cloud. Enterprises today want to build their applications in a more cloud native way and dynamic to get the most from these tools spanning across multiple cloud vendors.

This chapter looks at multi cloud set up with AWS and Google Cloud. If you already have workloads running in AWS in your EKS cluster and want to explore Google Kubernetes Engine (GKE) as part of your ongoing modernisation strategy, you can leverage Google Anthos to port GKE on AWS.

In this chapter, we will demonstrate how you can setup and deploy workloads on GKE in AWS and manage it from Google GKE dashboard. We will also demonstrate how you can attach your existing EKS cluster and make it part of Google Kubernetes cluster ecosystem. This can also enable you to leverage Google Anthos Config Management service to configure and manage workloads between AWS and Google Kubernetes clusters.

ANTHOS GKE ON AWS

Anthos offers a multi cloud solution by way of extending its native Google Cloud based GKE cluster to AWS environment. In this section, we will demonstrate how you can setup GKE cluster on AWS and manage it via Anthos dashboard.

Architecture for GKE on AWS

A GKE cluster on AWS is also called Anthos cluster on AWS. The architecture building blocks of Anthos cluster on AWS consist of two primary components:

- A management service cluster

- A user cluster

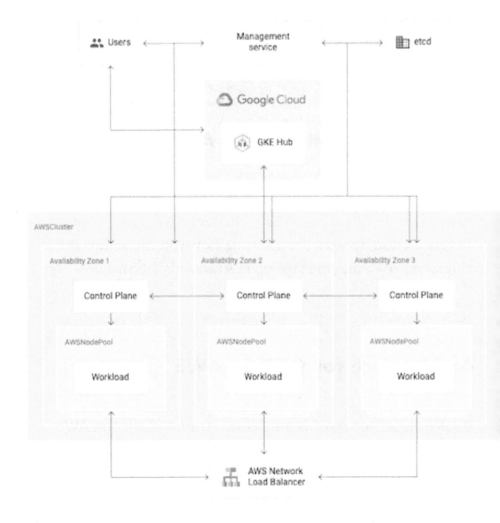

Figure 7.1 - GKE ON AWS (Architecture Image from Google Cloud Documentation)

A management service cluster is a meta control plane that allows you to create and manage user cluster control plane and nodes. User cluster is basically a GKE cluster where the application workload runs.

Management service cluster runs a Kubernetes operator that embodies a controller that manages the lifecycle of the GKE cluster via AWS APIs. It allows you to create, update and delete the GKE cluster on AWS.

The management service cluster is provisioned via terraform in either a new or existing VPC in a single availability zone. It must always be present in the same VPC as your user cluster. The management cluster is a single node EC2 instance that can manage multiple user clusters. The instance itself is part of a private subnet.

The user cluster represents custom resources *AWSCluster* and *AWSNodePool* with its Custom Resource Definitions (CRDs) provisioned in management service cluster. The *AWSCluster* represents control plane and *AWSNodePool* are worker nodes part of the node pool. The node pool concept is similar to that of GKE node pools where nodes in the pool have similar resource configuration. The placement of the user cluster across zones is determined when you create the management service cluster. It is typically placed across three availability zones for higher availability (HA). The management service cluster provisions the user cluster in a private subnet. It communicates with the user cluster control plane via TCP based AWS Network Load Balancer (NLB).

The cluster nodes both management service and user, are backed by auto scaling groups that ensure a certain minimum level of nodes always running in the event of node failure. Each control plane store cluster data in the local *etcd* database.

Before you setup GKE on AWS, the following prerequisites must be in place:

- AWS CLI is configured with the user having admin privileges

- Two AWS KMS keys. Keys are required to encrypt application secrets and the service management cluster data stored at rest with *etcd* database.

- Three Google service accounts with the following roles: gkehub.admin, serviceusage.serviceUsageViewer (To manage Hub memberships) gkehub.connect (to setup Connect agent for your user clusters) storage.objectViewer (to access Container Registry) Download the JSON keys for the above service accounts in particular folder. It will be later needed when configuring management service cluster

- Terraform (preferably latest version)

- *kubectl* Kubernetes client tool

As a first step, download the Anthos GKE tool – *anthos-gke*. This tool is required to setup the management service cluster.

```
gsutil cp gs://gke-multi-cloud-release/aws/
aws-1.9.1-gke.0/bin/linux/amd64/anthos-gke . [for
Linux]
```

```
gsutil cp gs://gke-multi-cloud-release/aws/
aws-1.9.1-gke.0/bin/darwin/amd64/anthos-gke . [for
Mac]
```

Download the tool using the above URL based on your operating environment. After the download is complete, you can make the file executable using the following command and put it in the folder that is available in the OS path, like */usr/local/bin*

```
chmod 755 anthos-gke
```

Creating and Configuring Management Service Cluster

The management service cluster is created using Kubernetes manifest YAML file that defines the custom resource called *AWSManagementService*.

Let's create the file and understand the configuration that you will provide:

```yaml
#anthos-gke.yaml
apiVersion: multicloud.cluster.gke.io/v1
kind: AWSManagementService
metadata:
  name: management
spec:
  version: aws-1.9.1-gke.0
  region: ap-south-1
  authentication:
    awsIAM:
      adminIdentityARNs:
      - arn:aws:iam::79X531X0XX29:user/anthosdev
    kmsKeyARN: arn:aws:kms:ap-south-1:XXX1306129:key/
12d39a92-688b-XX40-b69c-720e50c4cb74
    databaseEncryption:
      kmsKeyARN: arn:aws:kms:ap-
south-1:XXX3130XX29:key/79bc4275-c292-4af3-871b-
XXX90b4d5ec7
    googleCloud:
      projectID: <your_google_project>
      serviceAccountKeys:
        managementService: gke-hub-key.json
        connectAgent: gke-connect-key.json
        node: gke-storage-key.json
    dedicatedVPC:
```

```
vpcCIDRBlock: 172.30.0.0/16
availabilityZones:
- ap-south-1a
privateSubnetCIDRBlocks:
- 172.30.0.0/24
publicSubnetCIDRBlocks:
- 172.31.0.0/24
# Optional
bastionHost:
  allowedSSHCIDRBlocks:
  - 0.0.0.0/0
```

The above manifest yaml uses a custom resource named *AWSManagementService* that represents the management service cluster. It is part of *ap-south-1* (Mumbai) region. You have to specify the Amazon Resource Name (ARN) of the user with admin capabilities that will be responsible to create this cluster. The cluster will use two AWS KMS key ARN, one each to encrypt data during installation and the *etcd* database. All the cluster details and meta data is stored in the *etcd* database.

The cluster node will be setup in a dedicated VPC in a single availability zone in a private subnet. For the production environment, you may want to set this up in three availability zones for HA, but we will keep it simple here and configure it in a single zone. You also specify CIDRs for private and public subnets.

The above manifest will also create a bastion host in a public subnet, which we will keep it accessible by anyone (0.0.0.0/0). The bastion host will be used to connect and access the management service cluster. You will also provide the earlier created service account JSON keys to manage the Hub and Connect agent.

Before applying the above manifest file, you will initialise the process to validate the above manifest file with the following command:

```
anthos-gke aws management init
```

```
Output:
```

```
generating cluster ID
using default bootstrap S3 bucket name: gke-anthos-
book-322415-ap-south-1-bootstrap
encrypting Google Cloud service account key
(Management Service)
encrypting Google Cloud service account key (Connect
Agent)
encrypting Google Cloud service account key (Node)
generating root certificate authority (CA)
generating RSA private key for Kubernetes service
account signer
writing file: anthos-gke.status.yaml
```

The above command also encrypts the service account JSON keys provided earlier apart from setting up Certificate Authority (CA) and generating private key to sign Kubernetes based service accounts. The configuration is saved in the *anthos-gke.status.yaml* file.

You will now create the management service cluster by applying the *anthos-gke.yaml* manifest file created earlier.

```
anthos-gke aws management apply
```

The above command bootstraps the creation of a cluster environment on AWS using Terraform. It sets up the underlying cluster infrastructure through the use of Terraform. The infrastructure will contain a dedicated VPC with a private and public subnet. It will create two EC2 instances, one will be a cluster node in a private subnet and the other will be a bastion host on a public subnet. The cluster node or the management instance will be part of the autoscaling group that will ensure that 1 instance will always be available all the time.

Further, it will create an internal TCP based Network Load Balancer to access the cluster API server on port 443. It will also create necessary security groups to provide for appropriate firewall boundaries.

	Name		Instance ID	Instance state		Instance type		Status check
☐	gke-b02e6ce9-management-0	▽	I-0a1f8df425c0583ac	⊘ Running	⊕⊖	t3.medium	▽	⊘ 2/2 checks passed
☐	gke-b02e6ce9-bastion		I-052ead2fef69cedbe	⊘ Running	⊕⊖	t3.medium		⊘ 2/2 checks passed

It is important to note that the management service cluster is just one EC2 instance that operates as a control plane node. At the heart of this control plane node is the static pod named *gke-aws-cluster-operator* that runs *gke-aws-node-agent-binary* that facilitates management operations on GKE (user) cluster. The said binary itself can be found in the S3 bucket named *gke-anthos-book-322415-ap-south-1-bootstrap*.

Connecting to Management Service Cluster

The management cluster node EC2 instance sits in a private subnet and therefore not directly accessible from outside of VPC. You will have to use a bastion host to connect and access management instance. The bastion host is not needed if you have a direct or dedicated connectivity like VPN or AWS Direct Connect.

The terraform output file *outputs.tf* has the necessary script to connect to the bastion host. You will use the *terraform* client tool to output the generated script to a file named *bastion-tunnel.sh* and execute that file to create a SSH tunnel to the bastion host.

```
terraform output bastion_tunnel > bastion-tunnel.sh
chmod 755 bastion-tunnel.sh
```

Execute the *bastion-tunnel.sh* script file to open the tunnel to the bastion host.

```
./bastion-tunnel.sh -N -4
```

The above command will perform SSH to bastion host with relevant options. Here the -N indicates that the remote command should not be executed and simply perform port forwarding. The -4 option indicates mandatory use of IPv4 address only. The command will block and keep the terminal session open.

You will now generate credentials as part of kube config to authenticate against management service cluster. You will use *anthos-gke* tool to fetch the credentials for the management cluster.

```
anthos-gke aws management get-credentials
```

The bastion EC2 instance hosts a forward proxy runtime that listens on port *8118*. This proxy runtime forwards any command issued to the management service cluster API server. Now as we have already configured the credentials for our cluster, let's interact with the cluster through this proxy runtime.

```
env HTTPS_PROXY=http://localhost:8118 \
```

```
kubectl cluster-info
```

Open another terminal and execute the above Kubernetes command. The command will go via proxy server and execute on the management service cluster. It will simply fetch the cluster information.

Let's explore one more command.

```
env HTTPS_PROXY=http://localhost:8118 \
  kubectl get crds
```

Output:

```
NAME    CREATED AT
awsclusters.multicloud.cluster.gke.io
2021-11-18T11:30:56Z
awsnodepools.multicloud.cluster.gke.io
2021-11-18T11:30:56Z
```

The above command will display the CRDs for the GKE cluster (*AWSCluster*) and its node pool (*AWSNodePool*). In the next section, you will use the management service cluster to create and configure the GKE cluster on AWS using the the *AWSCluster* and *AWSNodePool* custom resources.

Creating and Configuring GKE (User) Cluster

You will now use the management service cluster to create the GKE user cluster. The template content of the *AWSCluster* and *AWSNodePool* custom resources is already generated in the terraform output file *outputs.tf*. You will use the terraform client tool to output the generated template content to a file named *gke-cluster.yaml*.

```
terraform output cluster_example > gke-cluster.yaml
```

Below is the content of the *gke-cluster.yaml* output file.

gke-cluster.yaml

```
apiVersion: multicloud.cluster.gke.io/v1
kind: AWSCluster
metadata:
  name: cluster-0
spec:
  region: ap-south-1
  authentication:
    awsIAM:
      adminIdentityARNs:
      - arn:aws:iam::798531306129:user/anthosdev
```

```yaml
networking:
  vpcID: vpc-0d32e7545c65773dc
  serviceAddressCIDRBlocks:
  - 10.1.0.0/16
  podAddressCIDRBlocks:
  - 10.2.0.0/16
  serviceLoadBalancerSubnetIDs:
  - subnet-04fd1f44a71e1655c
  - subnet-0e819f1fab1c4f9c2
controlPlane:
  version: 1.17.9-gke.2801
  keyName: gke-b02e6ce9-keypair
  instanceType: t3.medium
  iamInstanceProfile: gke-b02e6ce9-controlplane
  securityGroupIDs:
  - sg-0798f3cf31e3b107e
  subnetIDs:
  - subnet-04fd1f44a71e1655c
  rootVolume:
    sizeGiB: 10
  etcd:
    mainVolume:
      sizeGiB: 10
  databaseEncryption:
    kmsKeyARN: arn:aws:kms:ap-south-1:9985710619:key/79bc4275-c292-4af3-871b-16890n4d5ec7
  hub:
```

```yaml
    membershipName: projects/anthos-book-322415/
locations/global/memberships/cluster-0
---
apiVersion: multicloud.cluster.gke.io/v1
kind: AWSNodePool
metadata:
  name: cluster-0-pool-0
spec:
  clusterName: cluster-0
  version: 1.17.9-gke.2801
  region: ap-south-1
  subnetID: subnet-04fd1f44a71e1655c
  minNodeCount: 3
  maxNodeCount: 5
  instanceType: t3.medium
  keyName: gke-bx2x6ce9-keypair
  iamInstanceProfile: gke-b02c6cv9-nodepool
  maxPodsPerNode: 100
  securityGroupIDs:
  - sg-0798f3xf3be3b107e
  rootVolume:
    sizeGiB: 10
```

As you can see from the above file, the infrastructure of the user cluster and its node pool is derived from the service management cluster. It uses the same VPC and availability zone. You can of course customise the configuration of the user cluster according to your requirement.

Apply the above file with the following command:

```
env HTTPS_PROXY=http://localhost:8118 \
  kubectl apply -f gke-cluster.yaml
```

As you can see, you are still using the same proxy runtime to forward the command to the management service control plane. The management service cluster will in turn create the user cluster and node pools.

You can check the status of the user cluster with the following command:

```
env HTTPS_PROXY=http://localhost:8118 \
  kubectl get AWSClusters
```

Output:

```
NAME        STATE         AGE   VERSION
ENDPOINT
cluster-0   Provisioning  17s   1.17.9-gke.2801
gke-674683a7-controlplane-41f6ba66fd13f57d.elb.ap-
south-1.amazonaws.com
```

The above command displays the user cluster status. It is still in the **Provisioning** state. It takes some time before the cluster turns into **Provisioned** state.

Connecting and Accessing GKE (User) Cluster

You will now generate credentials as part of kube config to authenticate against user cluster. You will use *anthos-gke* tool to fetch the credentials for the user cluster named *cluster-0*.

```
env HTTPS_PROXY=http://localhost:8118 \
  anthos-gke aws clusters get-credentials cluster-0
```

Once you are connected with the GKE cluster, you will see there is one extra namespace named *gke-connect* apart from regular Kubernetes namespaces.

```
env HTTPS_PROXY=http://localhost:8118 \
  kubectl get ns
```
Output:

```
NAME            STATUS    AGE
default         Active    17h
```

```
gke-connect          Active   16h
kube-node-lease      Active   17h
kube-public          Active   17h
kube-system          Active   17henv
```

```
HTTPS_PROXY=http://localhost:8118 \
  kubectl get pods -n gke-connect
```

Output:

```
NAME
READY   STATUS    RESTARTS    AGE
gke-connect-agent-20211112-00-00-fd886b774-zk2n5
1/1     Running   0           17h
```

The *gke-connect* namespace will host the Connect Agent pod that is responsible to connect with the GKE Hub back in the Google Cloud. This will enable you to view your cluster in the Anthos and GKE dashboard from the Google Cloud as shown in figure 7.2.

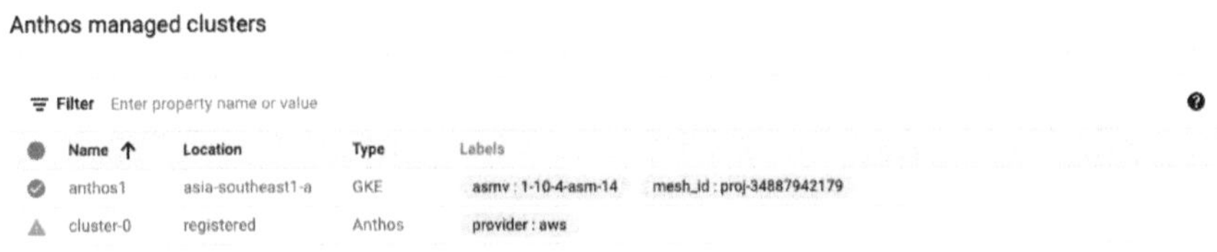

Figure 7.2 - Anthos Cluster Dashboard

As you can see from the figure 7.2, the Google Cloud Anthos dashboard now displays our AWS cluster **cluster-0**. The label **provider:aws** indicates the AWS cluster registered with the Hub. But if you see the above image, the cluster has a yellow warning icon that indicates you have to login into the cluster before we can actually see the workloads in action.

Logging in to the cluster

In order for the Anthos to gain visibility into AWS GKE cluster, you must login into the registered AWS cluster using Kubernetes based secret token that has permission to read cluster nodes. As a first step, you will create a Kubernetes service account.

```
env HTTPS_PROXY=http://localhost:8118 \
    kubectl create serviceaccount -n kube-system admin
```

The above command will create the service account named *admin* as part of *kube-system* namespace. This will also create the secret token of the admin service account in the said namespace. You can view the secrets by running the following command:

```
kubectl get secrets -n kube-system
```

Output:

```
NAME
TYPE                                             DATA    AGE
admin-token-vdbg7
kubernetes.io/service-account-token    3       39s
attachdetach-controller-token-ws58f
kubernetes.io/service-account-token    3       22h
aws-cloud-provider-token-s9zfz
kubernetes.io/service-account-token    3       22h
calico-kube-controllers-token-4b95q
kubernetes.io/service-account-token    3       22h
calico-node-token-9szbk
kubernetes.io/service-account-token    3       22h
....
```

Now you will bind the admin service account with the
predefined cluster role named *cluster-admin*. The cluster-
admin role has all the admin level privileges to operate on the
cluster.

```
env HTTPS_PROXY=http://localhost:8118 \
   kubectl create clusterrolebinding admin-role-
binding \
   --clusterrole cluster-admin --serviceaccount kube-
system:admin
```

The above command will make sure that the admin service account is able to view, read and operate on the cluster nodes. Now you grab the secret token of this service account and provide this to Anthos as part of the login process.

```
env HTTPS_PROXY=http://localhost:8118 \
  kubectl get secret admin-token-vdbg7 -n kube-system
-o jsonpath='{$.data.token}' | base64 -D
```

Output:

tpZCI6Inh0YTByc2h5TDVBSFU0cTdHRVFkMDdWSm94Ty1tMkVlLX
ZRdGJlZmNKWDQifQ.eyJpc3MiOiJrdWJJ......v1x3w4IB8nb

You already know the name of the secret from the earlier command. You get the data of that secret which is encoded as base64 and decode it. It will print the decoded data (see the above output).

You will now copy the above decoded secret data and paste it while performing login into the registered AWS GKE cluster from the Anthos dashboard.

Click on the LOGIN button and chose **Token** as an authentication method as shown in figure 7.3. Paste the decoded secret data and perform login. You will be now logged into the cluster. It effectively means that you can now see your application workloads from the Google Cloud GKE dashboard.

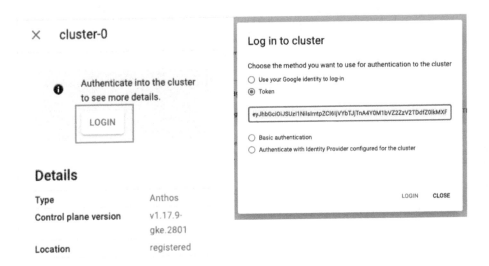

Figure 7.3 - Login to Cluster Option

You will now create a sample application and view it from the GKE dashboard.

Creating Sample Application

Now that our AWS GKE cluster **cluster-0** is registered and you are logged in as an admin user, you will now deploy a sample hello world application. For this use case, we will take a readily available hello world image from the Google Registry (gcr.io).

The following command will deploy and scale our hello world application to 3 replicas.

```
env HTTPS_PROXY=http://localhost:8118 \
  kubectl create deploy hello-world --image gcr.io/
google-samples/hello-app:2.0
```

```
env HTTPS_PROXY=http://localhost:8118 \
  kubectl scale deploy hello-world --replicas 3
```

The above command will create three pods for the *hello-world* deployment. Let's first verify using the CLI.

```
env HTTPS_PROXY=http://localhost:8118 \

kubectl get pods
```

Output:

```
NAME                             READY   STATUS
RESTARTS    AGE
hello-world-6f5db8b975-92pgl     1/1     Running
0           5s
hello-world-6f5db8b975-jhlm9     0/1
ContainerCreating    0           5s
hello-world-6f5db8b975-xjnxq     1/1     Running
0           70s
```

As our AWS GKE cluster is equipped with the Connect Agent pod, this will enable you to view the AWS cluster workloads from the Google Cloud GKE dashboard.

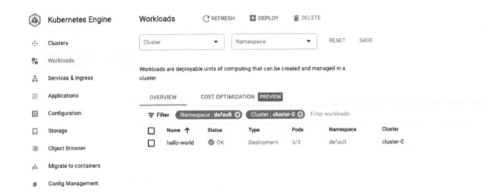

Figure 7.4 - Workloads showing sample application

As you can see, it is so seamless to create and manage a GKE cluster on a different cloud provider like AWS. The experience is similar to that of managing a native GKE cluster on Google Cloud.

In the next section, you will look at how to attach an existing AWS EKS cluster to Anthos environment.

INTEGRATING AWS EKS WITH ANTHOS

Anthos allows you to attach any non-GKE Kubernetes cluster. In this section, we will demonstrate how to attach an existing

AWS EKS cluster and make it part of Anthos ecosystem. Once the cluster is attached, you can view and manage it from the Anthos dashboard in the Google Cloud Console. You can also enable features like Anthos Config Management (ACM) to your AWS EKS cluster and apply policies across your environment for compliance and governance. The AWS EKS cluster will show up as an external cluster alongside other GKE clusters in the Anthos dashboard.

To attach the AWS EKS cluster, make sure you have the following prerequisites in place:

- AWS EKS cluster with Kubernetes version 1.19, 1.20 or 1.21

- Anthos Environment - Please refer to *Anthos Installation* chapter for setup details.

We need to perform the following steps to attach the AWS EKS cluster

- Enable relevant APIs

- Creating Service Account

- Registering the Cluster

- Login into the Registered AWS Cluster

Enable APIs

As a first step, you will enable relevant APIs that will allow you to connect and register your cluster with the Hub a.k.a project fleet that will make the cluster part of Anthos ecosystem.

Replace PROJECT_ID, with your own Google Cloud project id. The following commands enables the necessary APIs:

```
gcloud services enable \
--project=[PROJECT_ID] \
container.googleapis.com \
gkeconnect.googleapis.com \
gkehub.googleapis.com \
cloudresourcemanager.googleapis.com \
iam.googleapis.com
```

Creating Service Account

As a second step, you will create a service account that will be used by AWS EKS cluster to authenticate against Anthos.

```
gcloud iam service-accounts create gke-anthos --
project=${PROJECT_ID}

gcloud projects add-iam-policy-binding ${PROJECT_ID}
\
```

```
--member="serviceAccount:gke-anthos@$
{PROJECT_ID}.iam.gserviceaccount.com" \
--role="roles/owner"

gcloud iam service-accounts keys create gke-anthos-
key.json \
--iam-account=gke-anthos@$
{PROJECT_ID}.iam.gserviceaccount.com \
--project=${PROJECT_ID}
```

The above command creates a service account named *gke-anthos* and is assigned the *owner* role that grants full admin access to the said account. For our use case here, we are simplifying the access privilege by granting the *owner* permission. But in an ideal world, granting owner role is not recommended and the principle of least privilege should be followed when granting permissions to users or service accounts.

The last command will create and download the JSON key for the said service account. You will use this JSON key while registering the AWS EKS cluster. The JSON key will be used to authenticate the AWS EKS cluster with Anthos.

Registering the Cluster

You will now register the AWS EKS cluster with the project fleet that will allow you to view and manage the cluster from the Anthos console dashboard.

```
gcloud container hub memberships register aws \
--context=rn:aws:eks:ap-
south-1:798531306129:cluster/aws-cluster \
--kubeconfig=~/.kube/config \
-service-account-key-file=gke-anthos-key.json
```

The above command registers the AWS EKS cluster and creates a membership named *aws*. The command expects kube config and the context name of the AWS cluster. If you do not create the context for the AWS cluster then by default the context is the cluster's Amazon Resource Name (ARN). Upon registration, it will install the Connect Agent on the cluster that will enable you to view and manage your cluster from the Anthos and GKE dashboard. The Connect Agent pod will be part of the *gke-connect* namespace. The Connect Agent will authenticate to Google using the earlier generated service account JSON key. Registering a cluster indicates that the cluster is now in the realm of Anthos ecosystem.

You can view the registered clusters by giving the following command:

```
gcloud container hub memberships list
```

Output:

```
NAME         EXTERNAL_ID
anthos       158999b6-5e01-4f55-9314-148aac98345d
aws-cluster  1245479d-7886-4cf2-91c3-0363fc114910
```

The view from the console looks like the following as shown in figure 7.5.

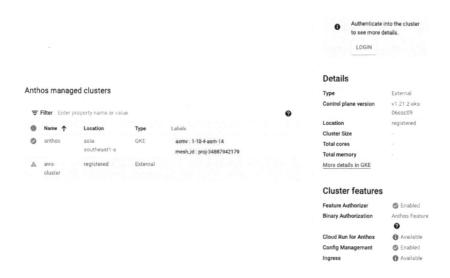

Figure 7.5: AWS Cluster in Anthos Dashboard

As you can see in figure 7.5, the attached AWS cluster is tagged as **External** which means it is a non-GKE cluster. You will also see an already existing GKE cluster (if you have already created one).

If you select the AWS cluster and observe the right side panel, you will see it still does not show the memory and CPU values of the cluster. So at this point Anthos does not have the visibility into the AWS EKS cluster. To get the cluster visibility, you will have to login to the cluster.

Login into the Registered AWS Cluster

In order for the Anthos to gain visibility into AWS EKS cluster, you must login into the registered AWS cluster using Kubernetes based secret token that has permission to read cluster nodes. As a first step, create a Kubernetes *ClusterRole* resource that will have all the permissions to read the cluster nodes.

```
apiVersion: rbac.authorization.k8s.io/v1
kind: ClusterRole
metadata:
  name: cluster-node-reader
rules:
- apiGroups: [""]
  resources: ["nodes"]
  verbs: ["get", "list", "watch"]
```

Connect to your AWS EKS cluster and apply the above YAML. It will create a *ClusterRole* resource by the name *cluster-node-reader*. You will now bind this role to the service account by creating *ClusterRoleBinding* resource.

Let's first create a Kubernetes service account.

```
kubectl create serviceaccount anthos
```

The above command will create the service account by the name anthos. This will also create the secret token of the anthos service account. You can view the secrets by running the following command:

```
kubectl get secrets
```

```
Output:
```

```
NAME                    TYPE
DATA    AGE
anthos-token-bxktd      kubernetes.io/service-account-
token   3       8m17s
default-token-2nxvq     kubernetes.io/service-account-
token   3       3d6h
```

Now you will bind the anthos service account with the earlier create cluster role *cluster-node-reader*.

```
kubectl create clusterrolebinding anthos-cluster-
node-reader-binding --clusterrole cluster-node-
reader --serviceaccount default:anthos
```

The above command will make sure that the anthos service account is able to view and read the cluster nodes. Now you grab the secret token of this service account and provide this to Anthos as part of the login process.

```
kubectl get secret anthos-token-bxktd -o
jsonpath='{$.data.token}' | base64 -D
Output:
```

xxxhbGciOiJSUzI1NiIsImtpZCI6IjVYbTJjTnA4Y0M1bVZ2ZzV2
TDdfZ0lkMXFEOWtIWFh1THotdUpUVHJO..bmLHuc9ARHklXMLzzz

You already know the name of the secret from the earlier command. You get the data of that secret which is encoded as base64 and decode it. It will print the decoded data (see the above output).

You will now copy the above decoded secret data and paste it while performing login into the registered AWS cluster from the Anthos cluster dashboard.

Click on the LOGIN button and chose **Token** as an authentication method as shown in figure 7.6. Paste the decoded secret data and perform login.

Figure 7.6 - Login to Cluster Option

You will now see the AWS EKS cluster resource details like memory and CPU.

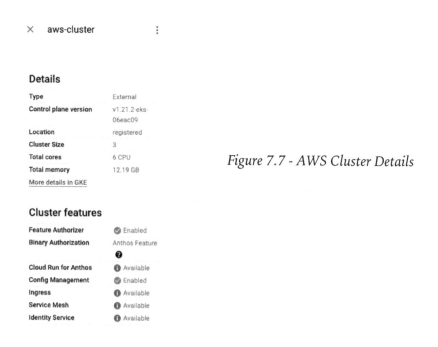

Figure 7.7 - AWS Cluster Details

Anthos now has visibility into the AWS EKS cluster and displays the cluster size, total CPU cores and memory.

As you can see, it is so easy to make existing non-GKE cluster part of Anthos ecosystem. Going ahead you could use features like ACM to automate the deployment in a multi cluster environment.

SUMMARY

In this chapter, you got the handle on key business drivers to adopt a multi cloud strategy. You then learned how you can install and setup a GKE cluster in the AWS environment. You also saw sample application deployment to the AWS GKE cluster The application workloads can be viewed and managed from the Google Cloud GKE dashboard. The chapter also walked you through attaching a non-GKE cluster like AWS EKS and making it part of Anthos ecosystem.

In the next chapter, you will look at implementing the CI/CD process with Anthos.

Note: A new version of Anthos clusters on AWS is generally available as of December 2. We will soon revise the content and update.

CHAPTER 8 : CI/CD WITH ANTHOS

INTRODUCTION

Continuous Integration and Continuous Delivery (CI/CD) is a practice or a process that consists of a set of tools and tasks to enable you to automate the process of building, testing, and deploying your applications in a repeatable manner across environments. CI/CD enables you to rapidly rollout releases of your application while it is being developed and maintained by teams that work in tandem to deliver reliable software across environments.

In this chapter, we will go through the details on how to build an automated CI/CD process for Anthos using a step by step approach.

In a traditional Information Technology (IT) landscape, you will often find two distinct teams operating independently viz. development and operations. The lack of coordination or collaboration among them gave rise to a new practice called DevOps. DevOps is a culture, methodology and set of tools that bridges the gap between development and operations teams. It has become an essential ingredient of modern day application development environment and process. The modern day software development teams are a bunch of agile devops engineers.

When you think about modernising your application platform, you think of building your software as containers and releasing them through a CI/CD process. A devops team can have resources functioning as developers and operators. While looking through the lens of devops, a developer develops, tests and builds the application into containers as deployable units and operators takes the deployment artifacts, applies configurations and security policies and performs deployments to the target runtime.

The security function can be clubbed with operations or it can be carved into a separate dedicated role that will be responsible for ensuring security and compliance of the application and the deployment environment.

ANTHOS CI/CD PROCESS WORKFLOW

Let's look at the workflow for Anthos CI/CD process.

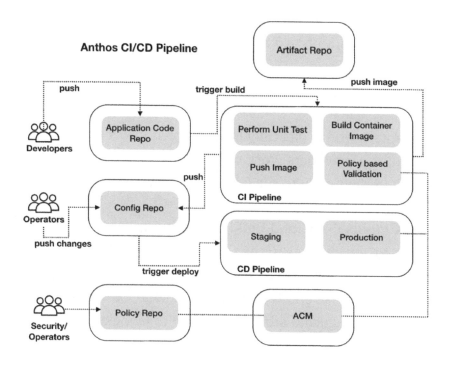

Figure 8.1 - CI/CD Workflow Process

With Anthos, you will follow a GitOps model to implement CI/CD processes.

All the application code, configuration files like Kubernetes manifests, security policy manifests and any customisation templates are stored in a Git source repository. The infrastructure setup is also configured as code or declarative constructs and stored in the source repository. The Git repository acts as a single source of truth that provides implicit built-in auditability for your application code, configurations and infrastructure code and a basis to propagate changes and drive deployment operations, governance and observability.

This concept of Git serving as an operating model to support software delivery lifecycle is referred to as GitOps.

At a high level, the process consist of the following -

- An application is basically broken down into a set of modules. Developers work on the respective modules and check in their code to the Git source repository.

- The CI tools like Cloud Build or Jenkins are configured to listen to any changes in the Git source repository. The changes could be a code commit to a particular branch, tagging a release etc. It then tests the code, builds the container image and stores the image to Google Container Registry or Artifact Registry.

- Once the container image is pushed to the container registry, the config files are updated with the new image URL. The operations team also uses Git to store all the configuration like Kubernetes manifests, security policy manifests and infrastructure code like terraform scripts. The declarative code is usually templatized using tools and best practices which is then applied for deployment across environments.

- The template files provide placeholders for injecting property values at runtime (like replicas : 2 for development and replicas : 5 for production). Tools such as Kustomize or Helm can be used to create templates for your manifests, without changing the original base manifest (YAML) files. Anthos provides integration with various such open source packaging and customisation tools implemented as part of best practices.

- The changes from earlier steps are reviewed, approved and then merged into the respective branch in that environment. Once the code is merged, the CD tools like Cloud Build picks up the changes from that branch and applies the configuration for deployment to the respective GKE environment.

- The operations or security team stores the governance or security policy configurations in the Git. The ACM component of Anthos can be used to enforce these policies to multiple GKE clusters across environments.

- Once the application is up and running, you can leverage ASM to gain more visibility into your services and benchmark its performances by defining Service Level Objective (SLO) in alignment with your application requirements. We had gone through the SLO concepts in the ASM chapter. For more details on SLO, you can refer to the Google SRE handbook at https://sre.google/books/.

The above process briefly outlines the workflow required to execute your CI/CD process across environments. In the next section, you will realise the workflow by setting up and executing the end-to-end CI/CD process for Anthos.

To demonstrate the CI/CD use case, we will take a two step approach. We will first perform the CI/CD process by testing the build and deploy scripts manually. This will help you understand the flow in its entirety.

Once all the manual steps are working, the second step will be to automate the flow using triggers and execute the CI/CD process end-to-end.

ANTHOS CI/CD REPOSITORY SETUP

In this section, you will setup source repositories that will form the basis for the CI/CD process. The setup will consist of three source repositories, viz. Application, Config and Policy.

- **Application repository**: This repository contains the application source code, Docker file and build scripts for creating the container images and performing policy validation. The repository is located at - https://github.com/cloudsolutions-academy/anthos-demo-app

- **Config repository**: This repository contains the Kubernetes manifests template created using tools like Kustomize. The template files are realised into specific configuration based on the environment (like staging or production) and placed in a deployment directory of your choice as part of this repository. The directory name could be as simple as configs/ or the name could be based on the environment like staging/ or production/.

The repository also contains deployment scripts that can be used to apply the final configuration to the GKE clusters as part of deployment.

- **Policy repository** : The policy repository contains declarative programmable governance policies against which the cluster is validated for compliance. You will use ACM based constraints and constraint templates as part of policy configurations.

For our CI/CD setup, you will use Google Cloud Source Repositories as a source repository, Cloud Container Registry for storing the container images, Cloud Build for continuous integration and deployment and ACM for creating and validating governance based policy for cluster compliance.

Prerequisites

The setup assumes you have the following prerequisites in place

- Anthos cluster with ACM and Config Sync enabled

- Git client tool

For setting up Anthos, please refer to Chapter 2 - Anthos Installation.

Got to the command terminal window and enable the following Google Cloud service APIs for your google cloud project, if not already enabled.

```
gcloud services enable container.googleapis.com
cloudbuild.googleapis.com
sourcerepo.googleapis.com
containeranalysis.googleapis.com
```

Create and configure repositories in Cloud Source Repositories

Configure Git to use your email address and name.

```
git config --global user.email "YOUR_EMAIL_ADDRESS"
git config --global user.name "YOUR_NAME"
```

Please make sure the above user has the admin role to create and update repository. For more details on required roles, you can refer to *https://cloud.google.com/source-repositories/docs/ configure-access-control*

You will set up two source repositories - Application and Configuration.

• Create a top level directory inside your home directory

```
mkdir anthos-demo
cd anthos-demo
```

- To get started quickly, we have made the complete source code for the application and configuration available in *cloudsolutions-academy* GitHub repository. This will be the same code you will emulate while working with your own repository in Google Cloud. You can execute the following command to get the application source code from our *cloudsolutions-academy* GitHub repository.

```
git clone https://github.com/cloudsolutions-
academy/anthos-demo-app \
demo-app
```

- Execute the following command to get the configuration source files from our cloudsolutions-academy GitHub repository..

```
git clone https://github.com/cloudsolutions-
academy/anthos-demo-config \
demo-config
```

- Execute the following command to create the repository on Google Cloud.

```
gcloud source repos create demo-app
```

```
gcloud source repos create demo-config
```

- Configure the above two created repositories as remote.

```
cd ~/anthos-demo/demo-app

PROJECT_ID=$(gcloud config get-value project)

git remote add google \
    https://source.developers.google.com/p/$
{PROJECT_ID}/r/demo-app


cd ~/anthos-demo/demo-config

PROJECT_ID=$(gcloud config get-value project)

git remote add google-conf \
    https://source.developers.google.com/p/$
{PROJECT_ID}/r/demo-config
```

Sample Application

The sample code added to the demo-app repository is a simple Node.js application that consists of three endpoints, viz. /echo, /healthz and /fetchWebsite. The *echo* endpoint prints the message, the *healthz* endpoint checks application health and prints ok message, if it is healthy and *fetchWebsite* endpoint tests inbound and outbound connectivity to/from the GKE cluster by visiting a public website.

To view the code, change directory to *demo-app* and open the *server.js* file.

```
'use strict';

const express = require('express');
const request = require('request');
const bodyParser = require('body-parser');
const {Buffer} = require('safe-buffer');

const app = express();

app.set('case sensitive routing', true);
app.use(bodyParser.json());

const PORT = 8080;

app.post('/echo', (req, res) => {
  res
    .status(200)
    .json({message: req.body.message})
    .end();
});


app.get('/healthz', (req, res) => {
```

```
console.log(req.connection.remoteAddress);
res
    .status(200)
    .json({message: "ok"})
    .end();
});

app.get('/fetchWebsite', (req, res) => {

  request('https://navveenbalani.dev/', function
(error, response, html) {
    if (!error && response.statusCode == 200) {
      res
      .status(200)
      .json({message: "ok"})
      .end();
    } else {
      res
      .status(500)
      .json({message: error})
      .end(); }})});

  app.listen(PORT);
console.log(`Running on ${PORT}`);
```

The following shows the docker file for the application. It downloads the base node docker image and builds the application code and exposes the application on port *8080*.

```
FROM node:12
WORKDIR /usr/src/app
COPY package*.json ./
RUN npm install
COPY . .
EXPOSE 8080
CMD [ "npm", "start" ]
```

In the next section, you will kick start the process of executing the CI/CD process.

DEVELOPING THE CI/CD PROCESS

In this section, as part of the first step, you will use the manual approach to build and deploy the sample application using the Cloud Build scripts. This will also, in a way, test our scripts that it is performing as per the expectation. Later, as part of the *Setting up CI/CD Process* section we will automate the CI/CD process through these scripts using triggers.

Creating the Integration Pipeline

You will create the container image for the above application using Cloud Build and store the same in the Container Registry as part of the integration pipeline.

Following shows the listing of Cloud Build file: *app-build-trigger-ci.yaml* located in the *demo-app* directory.

```
steps:

 #Build the container image.
- name: 'gcr.io/cloud-builders/docker'
  id: Build
  args:
  - 'build'
  - '-t'
  - 'gcr.io/$PROJECT_ID/demoapp:$SHORT_SHA'
  - '.'


# Push image to gcr.io Container Registry
# The SHORT_SHA variable is automatically replaced
by Cloud Build.
- name: 'gcr.io/cloud-builders/docker'
  id: Push
  args:
  - 'push'
  - 'gcr.io/$PROJECT_ID/demoapp:$SHORT_SHA'
```

The SHORT_SHA is replaced with the commit SHA by the Cloud Build tool during runtime. You can test the above script by executing the following steps.

```
cd ~/anthos-demo/demo-app
```

```
COMMIT_ID="$(git rev-parse --short=7 HEAD)"

gcloud builds submit --config app-build.yaml .
--substitutions SHORT_SHA=${COMMIT_ID}
```

You should see the image getting built and pushed to the
container registry. You will receive a success message as shown
in the output below.

```
Finished Step #1 - "Push"
PUSH
DONE
6538933f-503a-4c92-ad62-ad6ecdae97a9
2021-12-20T11:14:06+00:00   43S        gs://anthos-
demo-335406_cloudbuild/source/
1639998843.535127-9568f800e88d410a9d7187f6363918c3.t
gz  -        SUCCESS
```

You can verify the image in the Container Registry, by
navigating to the Google Cloud Console *Navigation menu icon >
Container Registry -> Images*. The tag as shown in the figure 8.2
should match the latest COMMIT_ID that was passed to the
build command.

Figure 8.2 - Image Details

You will now push the code to the google cloud *demo-app* repository

```
cd ~/anthos-demo/demo-app

git push  --all google
```

The following shows the output of the above command.

```
git push --all google
Enumerating objects: 32, done.
Counting objects: 100% (32/32), done.
Delta compression using up to 8 threads
Compressing objects: 100% (15/15), done.
Writing objects: 100% (32/32), 6.71 KiB | 6.71 MiB/
s, done.
Total 32 (delta 17), reused 32 (delta 17), pack-
reused 0
```

```
remote: Resolving deltas: 100% (17/17)
To https://source.developers.google.com/p/anthos-
demo-xx/r/demo-app
 * [new branch]        main -> main
```

You will use the above build script later as part of the CI
pipeline automation.

In the next section, you will create the delivery pipeline that
will deploy the container image to the Anthos cluster in the
respective environment like staging or production.

Creating the Delivery Pipeline

You will create the delivery pipeline by writing the deployment
script using Cloud Build.

Following shows the listing of Cloud Build file: *app-deploy-
delivery.yaml* located in the *demo-config* directory.

```
cd ~/anthos-demo/demo-config

nano app-deploy-delivery.yaml

#Continuous Delivery Pipeline Template for
Staging Branch

steps:
```

```
# Replace CLOUDSDK_COMPUTE_ZONE and
CLOUDSDK_CONTAINER_CLUSTER with your
# zone and Anthos Cluster name.
- name: 'gcr.io/cloud-builders/kubectl'
  id: Deploy
  args:
  - 'apply'
  - '-f'
  - 'config/staging/kubernetes.yaml'
  env:
  - 'CLOUDSDK_COMPUTE_ZONE=asia-southeast1-a'
  - 'CLOUDSDK_CONTAINER_CLUSTER=anthos-
cluster'
```

In the above code, you can replace the zone and cluster name
as per your environment.

Now, check-in the code in Google Cloud *demo-config* repository
by issuing the following command.

```
cd ~/anthos-demo/demo-config

git checkout -b staging

git add .

git commit -m "Cluster and zone changes as per
environment"
```

```
git push --all google-conf
```

You will create a branch called staging to check-in the initial changes. Staging branch will be used for initial deployment and once everything is working, changes can be propagated to another environment like pre-production or production. You will then, say, create the production branch (using *git checkout -b production*) and push the required changes to the said branch. The pipeline for the staging environment can be emulated for the production environment.

The *config/staging/kubernetes.yaml* file path mentioned in the *app-deploy-delivery.yaml* is the application deployment config. The *kubernetes.yaml* file is generated from the *kubernetes.yaml.template* located in *demo-config/manifests* folder. The *kubernetes.yaml.template* file represents a base reference deployment template that is used to customise the actual configs based on the environment like staging, production etc. where it's being deployed.

The templates are used as a best practice base configuration, that allows you to bind values to parameters or variables to realise it into a specific environment based configuration.

Let's inspect the *kubernetes.yaml.template* file

```
# Sample Kubernetes Deployment Template
# The COMMIT SHA variable below would be replaced by
the committed build image
```

```
# as part of CD process.

apiVersion: apps/v1
kind: Deployment
metadata:
  name: demoapp
  labels:
    app: demoapp
    businessunit: software-demo
spec:
  replicas: 1
  selector:
    matchLabels:
      app: demoapp
  template:
    metadata:
      labels:
        app: demoapp
        businessunit: software-demo
    spec:
      containers:
      - name: demoapp
        image: gcr.io/GOOGLE_CLOUD_PROJECT/
demoapp:COMMIT_SHA
        ports:
        - containerPort: 8080
---
kind: Service
apiVersion: v1
```

```
metadata:
  name: demoapp
spec:
  selector:
    app: demoapp
  ports:
  - protocol: TCP
    port: 80
    targetPort: 8080
  type: LoadBalancer
```

The customisation happens as part of the delivery pipeline where the template - *kubernetes.yaml.template* is realised into *config/staging/kubernetes.yaml* file. In this case, the COMMIT_SHA variable as shown above is replaced by the container build image (i.e COMMIT_ID) that we described in the *Creating the Container Image* section. You can use tools like Kustomize for performing various customisations based on your requirement.

You will also see a *businessunit: software-demo* label that indicates the business unit that owns the deployment. We will later make this label a mandatory requirement and validate its presence as part of the ACM Policy configuration and validation.

The following build code carries out the customisation steps. The build first checks-out the *demo-config* branch, customises the *kubernetes.yaml.template* using *sed* command and copies the *kubernetes.yaml* to staging directory for deployment as part of staging branch.

```
# This step clones the demo-config repository and
checks out
# staging branch
- id: Clone demo environment repository
  name: 'gcr.io/cloud-builders/gcloud'
  entrypoint: /bin/sh
  args:
  - '-c'
  - |
    mkdir hydrated-manifests &&
    gcloud source repos clone demo-config && \
    cd demo-config && \
    git checkout staging && \
    git config user.email $(gcloud auth list --
filter=status:ACTIVE --format='value(account)')


#This step modifies the kubernetes template with
#image id commit details
#and copies the files to hydrated-manifests for
further processing.
- id: Generate manifest
  name: 'gcr.io/cloud-builders/gcloud'
  entrypoint: /bin/sh
  args:
  - '-c'
```

```
    - |
      sed "s/GOOGLE_CLOUD_PROJECT/${PROJECT_ID}/g"
demo-config/manifests/kubernetes.yaml.template | \
      sed "s/COMMIT_SHA/${SHORT_SHA}/g" > hydrated-
manifests/kubernetes.yaml



   # If all works well, this step copies the
kubernetes.yaml to the staging directory.
- id: 'Copy config'
  name: 'gcr.io/cloud-builders/gcloud'
  entrypoint: '/bin/sh'
  args: ['-c', '\cp -r hydrated-manifests/
kubernetes.yaml demo-config/config/staging/
kubernetes.yaml']

# This step pushes the kubernetes.yaml manifest to
demo-config staging branch
- id: Push manifest to demo-config staging branch
  name: 'gcr.io/cloud-builders/gcloud'
  entrypoint: /bin/sh
  args:
  - '-c'
  - |
    set -x && \
    cd demo-config && \
    git add config/staging/kubernetes.yaml && \
    git commit -m "Commit manifest for gcr.io/$
{PROJECT_ID}/demoapp:${SHORT_SHA}" && \
```

```
git push origin staging
```

Now, the next step is to integrate the above code, after the container image is deployed and pushed to the container registry. So let's combine the above code into a file named *app-build-trigger-cd.yaml* file. The *app-build-trigger-cd.yaml* file is already provided in *demo-config* directory for your reference.

```
cd ~/anthos-demo/demo-app/
```

```
nano app-build-trigger-cd.yaml
```

The following shows the high level snippet headers of combined listing in app-build-trigger-cd.yaml file.

```
steps:

#Build the container image.
#code ..

#Push image to gcr.io Container Registry
#code ..

#This step clones the demo-config repository  #and
checks out  staging branch
#code ..
```

```
#This step modifies the kubernetes template with
#image id commit details and copies the files to
hydrated-manifests for further processing.

# If all works well, this step copies the
kubernetes.yaml to staging directory.
#code ..

# This step pushes the kubernetes.yaml manifest to
demo-config staging branch
#code ..
```

Running the delivery pipeline

To run the above code, you will need to grant *the* required IAM role to the Cloud Build service account to commit changes to the *demo-config* repository and to deploy to the container.

You will perform the following steps to provide the required role.

```
PROJECT_NUMBER="$(gcloud projects describe $
{PROJECT_ID} --format='get(projectNumber)')"

echo $PROJECT_NUMBER
```

Set the following policies using the following command

```
gcloud projects add-iam-policy-binding ${PROJECT_NUMBER} \
    --member=serviceAccount:${PROJECT_NUMBER}@cloudbuild.gserviceaccount.com \
    --role=roles/container.developer --role=roles/source.writer
```

You should get the *Updated IAM Policy* message as shown in the output below.

```
Updated IAM policy for project [1264542XXX0].
bindings:
- members:
-serviceAccount:1264542XX@cloudbuild.gserviceaccount
.com
  role: roles/cloudbuild.builds.builder
....
```

Now, let's run the above code.

```
cd ~/anthos-demo/demo-app/

COMMIT_ID="$(git rev-parse --short=7 HEAD)"

gcloud builds submit --config app-build-trigger-cd.yaml . --substitutions SHORT_SHA=${COMMIT_ID}
```

You should see the success message being printed at the end as shown in the output below and the *kubernetes.yaml* file should be committed to the staging branch in the *demo-config* repository. You can verify the same at */config/staging* location.

```
Finished Step #5 - "Push manifest to demo-config
staging branch"
PUSH
DONE
ID  CREATE_TIME DURATION  SOURCE
IMAGES  STATUS
a6cb6feb-c1de-4288-8e3d-91f764bbb831
2021-12-20T12:54:31+00:00  55S       gs://anthos-
demo-335XX_cloudbuild/source/
1640004868.-22c3ba6a9467409d80069ef221fabc3f.tgz  -
SUCCESS
```

Now, let's run the delivery pipeline which should deploy the committed *kubernetes.yaml* in the staging environment of your cluster. The *git pull google staging* command below pulls the updated *kubernetes.yaml* file from the staging branch which is referenced in *app-deploy-delivery.yaml* file.

```
cd ~/anthos-demo/demo-config/

git pull google-conf staging
```

The following shows the output of the above command.

```
git pull google-conf staging
remote: Counting objects: 13, done
remote: Finding sources: 100% (5/5)
remote: Total 5 (delta 1), reused 5 (delta 1)
Unpacking objects: 100% (5/5), 815 bytes | 163.00
KiB/s, done.
From https://source.developers.google.com/p/anthos-
demo-335406/r/demo-config
 * branch              staging     -> FETCH_HEAD
   4714a0..0f8e49a   staging     -> google-conf/
staging
Updating 47140a0..0f8e49a
Fast-forward
 config/staging/kubernetes.yaml | 40 +++++++++++++++
++++++++++++++++++++++++++
 1 file changed, 40 insertions(+)
 create mode 100644 config/staging/kubernetes.yaml
```

Next, submit the build using the following command.

```
gcloud builds submit --config app-deploy-
delivery.yaml .
```

The following shows the output of the above command.

```
PUSH
```

```
DONE
ID                                          CREATE_TIME
DURATION  SOURCE
IMAGES  STATUS
6be8f0ba-f350-4e33-9532-7911b25ae7b4
2021-12-20T12:58:45+00:00   17S         gs://anthos-
demo-335406_cloudbuild/source/
1640005122.825047-19f0be88d8f64d9bbe0a0f1cd5ae7c51.t
gz    -          SUCCESS
```

Now, let's verify if the application was deployed and service is
created. Login to *Google Cloud Console -> Kubernetes Engine ->
Workloads* and you should see the *demoapp* listed as shown in
figure 8.3.

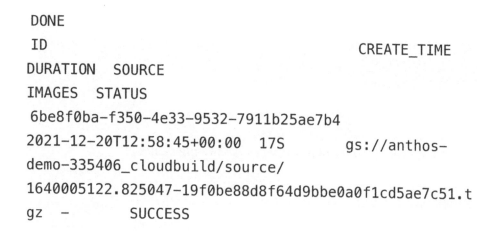

Figure 8.3 - Workloads showing demoapp

Click on *Services & Ingress* and you should see the *demoapp*
service running as shown in figure 8.4. Copy the IP address
from the Endpoint column.

Name ↑	Status	Type	Endpoints	Pods	Namespace	Clusters
canonical-service-controller-manager-metrics-service	✔ OK	Cluster IP	10.3.248.194	1/1	asm-system	anthos-cluster
canonical-service-controller-manager-metrics-service	✔ OK	Cluster IP	10.7.248.35	1/1	asm-system	sample-clust...
demoapp	✔ OK	External load balancer	34.126.168.187:80 ☒	1/1	default	anthos-cluster

Figure 8.4 - Services showing demoapp

Open the browser and navigate to URL *http://<your-endpoint-ip-addres>/healthz* or *http://<your-endpoint-ip-addres>/fetchWebsite* and you should see the below message being printed in browser, denoting the service was executed successfully.

```
{"message":"ok"}
```

Validate the Policy

As a next step, you will define a governance based policy to validate your configuration before it is deployed to the cluster as part of CI pipeline. The policy rule will check and enforce the use of *businessunit* label field in the deployment config.

The policy constraints definition is stored in the ACM repository located at - https://github.com/cloudsolutions-academy/anthos-demo-acm.git/. The cluster directory contains two files - *requiredlabels.yaml* and *deployment-must-have-businessunit.yaml*.

The *requiredlabels.yaml* file below is a constraint template defining our policy that expects a string array of labels as an input. If the input label is not present it will block the creation of deployment configuration. *For more details on how to create governance based programmable policies, refer to Chapter 6 - Anthos Config Management.*

```
apiVersion: templates.gatekeeper.sh/v1beta1
kind: ConstraintTemplate
metadata:
  name: k8srequiredlabels
spec:
  crd:
    spec:
      names:
        kind: K8sRequiredLabels
      validation:
        # Schema definition for the 'parameters'
field
        openAPIV3Schema:
          properties:
            labels:
              type: array
              items: string
```

```
targets:
  - target: admission.k8s.gatekeeper.sh
    rego: |
      package k8srequiredlabels

      violation[{"msg": msg, "details":
{"missing_labels": missing}}] {
          provided := {label |
input.review.object.metadata.labels[label]}
          required := {label | label :=
input.parameters.labels[_]}
          missing := required - provided
          count(missing) > 0
          msg := sprintf("The following label(s) are
required: %v", [missing])
      }
```

The above policy is then enforced as a constraint in the
deployment-must-have-businessunit.yaml file. The below constraint
applies a policy that mandates the use of labels *app* and
businessunit in the deployment configuration.

```
apiVersion: constraints.gatekeeper.sh/v1beta1
kind: K8sRequiredLabels
metadata:
  name: deployment-must-have-business-unit
spec:
  match:
```

```
kinds:
  - apiGroups: ["apps"]
    kinds: ["Deployment"]
parameters:
  labels: ["app", "businessunit"]
  message: "Deployment objects should have an
'businessunit' label indicating which business unit
owns it"
```

Now, let's integrate and validate the deployment against the above policy as part of the CI build process as shown below.

```
# This step fetches the policies from the Anthos
Config Management repository and consolidates every
resource in a single file.
- id: 'Download policies'
  name: 'gcr.io/kpt-dev/kpt'
  entrypoint: '/bin/sh'
  args: ['-c', 'kpt pkg get https://github.com/
cloudsolutions-academy/anthos-demo-acm.git/
cluster@main constraints
                && kpt fn source constraints/
hydrated-manifests/ > hydrated-manifests/kpt-
manifests.yaml']


# This step validates that all resources comply
with all policies.
- id: 'Validate against policies'
```

```
    name: 'gcr.io/config-management-release/policy-
controller-validate'
    args: ['--input', 'hydrated-manifests/kpt-
manifests.yaml']
```

Once the container image is pushed, it will validate the
configuration against the policy, prior to committing the
kubernetes.yaml file in the staging branch.

You will use *kpt* tool to fetch all the constraints from our ACM
repository at https://github.com/cloudsolutions-academy/
anthos-demo-acm.git. and consolidates the Kubernetes
configurations and the constraints in a single file named *kpt-
manifests.yaml*. The *kpt-manifests.yaml* file is then validated by the
policy controller to ensure all the constraints are met. The
deployment will fail when there is a violation of policy.

The updated CI pipeline with the above changes is made
available at app-build-trigger-acm-ci.yaml (in demo-app
repository).

The following shows the high level snippet headers of
combined listing for app-build-trigger-acm-ci.yaml.

```
steps:
 #Build the container image.
 # code …


 # Push image to gcr.io Container Registry
```

```
# code …

#This step clones the demo-config repository
# and checks out staging branch
# code …


#This step modifies the kubernetes template
#with #image id commit details and copies the
#files to hydrated-manifests for further
#processing.
# code …

# This step fetches the policies from the Anthos #
Config Management repository and consolidates  #
every resource in a single file.
# code ..

# This step validates that all resources comply #
with all policies.
# code ..

# If all works well, this step copies the        #
kubernetes.yaml to staging directory.
# code …

# This step pushes the kubernetes.yaml manifest # to
demo-config staging branch
# code ..
```

To run the above build, execute the following steps -

```
cd ~/anthos-demo/demo-app/

COMMIT_ID="test-$(git rev-parse --short=7 HEAD)"

gcloud builds submit --config app-build-trigger-acm-
ci.yaml . --substitutions SHORT_SHA=${COMMIT_ID}
```

You should receive a successful build message as shown in the output below.

```
Finished Step #7 - "Push manifest to demo-config
staging branch"
PUSH
DONE
ID                                        CREATE_TIME
DURATION   SOURCE
IMAGES   STATUS
67732e8a-0ffb-4362-9c50-4c141c7803c7
2021-12-20T13:44:30+00:00   1M5S       gs://anthos-
demo-x-cloudbuild/source/1640007867.806441-
xx8348bd4410dbb2dd55c.tgz   -        SUCCESS
```

So far, you have manually executed the CI/CD build process. In the next section, we will demonstrate how to setup an automated CI/CD process.

SETTING UP CI/CD PROCESS

To automate the CI/CD process, you will setup triggers.

Go to Google *Cloud Console -> Cloud Build - Triggers*. You will create two triggers, one for *app-build-trigger-acm-ci.yaml* (the CI part) and one for *app-deploy-delivery.yaml* (the CD part)

- Click on *Create Trigger* button

- Specify name as *App-CI*

- In the *Event*, keep the default *Push to Branch* option selected

- In the *Source*, specify the *demo-app* repository

- For the branch, specify main branch as wildcard pattern
  ^main$

- Keep the configuration as Cloud Build file

- In *Location*, specify the build file *app-build-trigger-acm-ci.yaml*

- Click *Create* button

The figure 8.5 show the above configuration details.

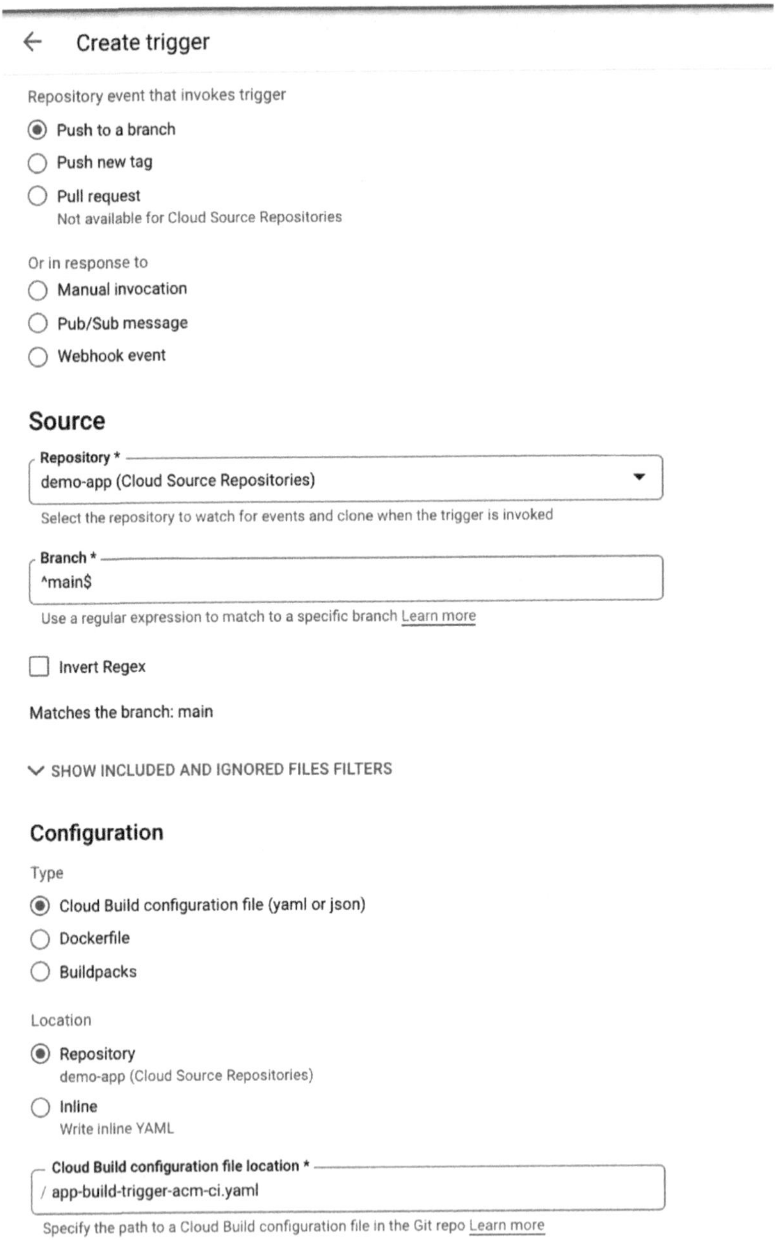

←   **Create trigger**

Repository event that invokes trigger

◉ Push to a branch

○ Push new tag

○ Pull request
    Not available for Cloud Source Repositories

Or in response to

○ Manual invocation

○ Pub/Sub message

○ Webhook event

Source

Repository *

demo-app (Cloud Source Repositories)   ▼

Select the repository to watch for events and clone when the trigger is invoked

Branch *

^main$

Use a regular expression to match to a specific branch Learn more

☐ Invert Regex

Matches the branch: main

⌄ SHOW INCLUDED AND IGNORED FILES FILTERS

Configuration

Type

◉ Cloud Build configuration file (yaml or json)

○ Dockerfile

○ Buildpacks

Location

◉ Repository
    demo-app (Cloud Source Repositories)

○ Inline
    Write inline YAML

Cloud Build configuration file location *

/ app-build-trigger-acm-ci.yaml

Specify the path to a Cloud Build configuration file in the Git repo Learn more

Figure 8.5 - Create Trigger for Continuous integration

With the above trigger configured, any commit to the application main branch will trigger the CI the execution pipeline. The pipeline will commit the *kubernetes.yaml* to the staging branch on successful execution.

Next step is to create a similar trigger on the staging branch which will execute the *app-deploy-delivery.yaml* file.

- Click on *Create Trigger* button

- Specify name as *App-CD*

- In the *Event*, keep the default *Push to Branch* option selected

- In the *Source*, specify the *demo-config* repository

- For the branch, specify main branch as wildcard pattern *^staging$*

- Keep the configuration as Cloud Build file

- In *Location*, specify the build file *app-deploy-delivery.yaml*

- Click *Create* button

The figure 8.6 show the above configuration details

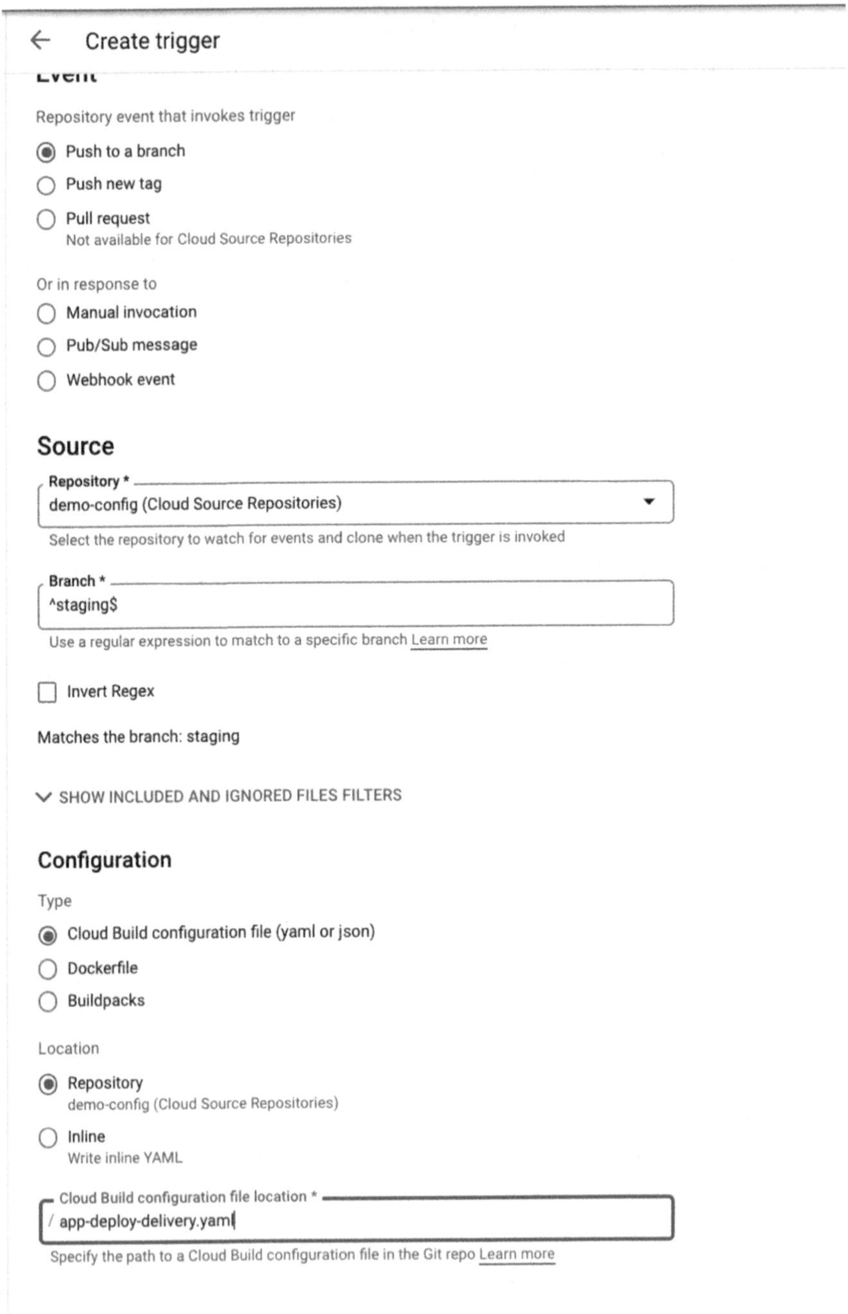

Event

Repository event that invokes trigger

⦿ Push to a branch

◯ Push new tag

◯ Pull request
Not available for Cloud Source Repositories

Or in response to

◯ Manual invocation

◯ Pub/Sub message

◯ Webhook event

Source

Repository *

demo-config (Cloud Source Repositories)   ▾

Select the repository to watch for events and clone when the trigger is invoked

Branch *

^staging$

Use a regular expression to match to a specific branch Learn more

☐ Invert Regex

Matches the branch: staging

⌄ SHOW INCLUDED AND IGNORED FILES FILTERS

Configuration

Type

⦿ Cloud Build configuration file (yaml or json)

◯ Dockerfile

◯ Buildpacks

Location

⦿ Repository
demo-config (Cloud Source Repositories)

◯ Inline
Write inline YAML

Cloud Build configuration file location *

/ app-deploy-delivery.yaml

Specify the path to a Cloud Build configuration file in the Git repo Learn more

Figure 8.6 - Create Trigger for Continuous delivery

You can now test the integrated CI/CD pipeline. Let's make some changes to *server.js* code.

```
cd ~/anthos-demo/demo-app
```

```
nano server.js
```

Replace the *ok* print message highlighted in bold with the *service is running* message as shown below.

```
app.get('/healthz', (req, res) => {
console.log(req.connection.remoteAddress);
res
    .status(200)
    .json({message: "ok"})
    .end();
});
```

by

```
app.get('/healthz', (req, res) => {
console.log(req.connection.remoteAddress);
res
    .status(200)
    .json({message: "server is running"})
    .end();
});
```

Save the file.

Commit the changes by executing the following commands.

```
git add .

git commit -m "Health service message changed"

git push --all google
```

Go to *Google Cloud Console -> Cloud Build -> History* and you should see the *App-CI* build being triggered as shown in the figure 8.7.

Figure 8.7 - Cloud Build History

Once the *App-CI* build is successfully executed as shown in figure 8.8 (see the green ticks), the *App-CD* pipeline will be triggered and the latest build will be deployed to the cluster in the staging environment.

Figure 8.8 - Cloud Build Submission Results

Open the URL *http://<your-endpoint-ip-addres>/healthz* in the browser and you should see the below latest message being printed.

```
{"message":"server is running"}
```

This completes the setup and execution of end to end CI/CD process for Anthos.

Now let's test the policy violation use case. You will remove the required *businessunit* label from the *kubernetes,template.yaml* file and in doing so, the build should fail as it violates our policy.

Follow the steps to modify the *kubernetes,template.yaml* file.

```
cd ~/anthos-demo/demo-config/
```

```
nano manifests/kubernetes.yaml.template
```

Just replace the label key *businessunit* with *businessunit1* in the file. Save the file.

Commit the changes by running the command

```
git add .

git commit —m "Negative policy test"

git push ——all google-conf
```

Go back to *Google Cloud Console. Go to Cloud Build -> Triggers* and click on *Run* on the *App-CI* row to run the build manually.

Figure 8.8 - Manually Run the Build

Go to History to see the build status. You would see the build failed at Step 5 - *Validate against policies* with the message as shown in the figure 8.9.

Figure 8.9 - Validate Policy Failed

```
"Step #5 - "Validate against policies": [error]
apps/v1/Deployment/demoapp : The following label(s)
are required: {"businessunit"}"
 Step #5 - "Validate against policies":
violatedConstraint: deployment-must-have-business-
unit
```

This test verifies our policy execution is working fine and the CI process fails due to violation of policy thereby changes are not committed to the staging branch.

SUMMARY

In this chapter, you learned the importance of DevOps and CI/CD as a practice. You learned how to build an end to end CI/CD process using step by step approach (from manual to automation).

You can further refine your CI/CD process as per your application release requirements. Things like adding unit tests, performing container image scanning, setting up more governance based policies and working with ACM components to enforce these policies and configurations on different clusters across environments.

WHAT'S NEXT

As this space is evolving rapidly, we would be constantly updating the book. All updates to the book will be delivered via Kindle so make sure you have auto updates turned on.

There are lot of capabilities that we plan to cover in our next release, such as Anthos Clusters on VMWare, Migrate for Anthos, comprehensive case studies / use cases on Anthos and extend our book to Google Distributed Cloud service that was announced in Google Next'21.

COMMENTS / SUGGESTIONS

Please share your suggestions/feedback to me@navveenbalani.dev or connect authors on Linkedin at https://www.linkedin.com/in/naveenbalani/ and https://www.linkedin.com/in/rajeev-hathi-963086bb/

The Anthos book is part of our *The Definitive Handbook* series. Our vision through the series is to enable our readers to understand the technology in simple terms and provide a go-to reference and a recipe for building any real-world application using the latest technology.

This is our fifth book in the series, the first being – *Enterprise IoT* which got acknowledged as one of the **Top Computing book for 2016** by *computingreview.com*.

We will also appreciate your support and subscription to the **YouTube channel - Cloud Solutions Academy**, where we host a range of topics on Anthos and technology in general. You can subscribe at the following URL.

https://www.youtube.com/c/CloudSolutionsAcademy

Made in the USA
Coppell, TX
11 February 2022